Rhonda Cobham was born and raised in Trinidad. She has lived and worked in the Caribbean, Britain, Nigeria and Germany. She now lives in the USA where she teaches Caribbean and African Literature and Feminist Theory at Amherst College.

Merle Collins is Grenadian. She studied at the University of the West Indies at Georgetown and holds a PhD in government from the London School of Economics. She is currently lecturing in Caribbean Studies at the Polytechnic of North London. A collection of her poetry, *Because the Dawn Breaks*, was published by Karia Press in 1985. She is also the author of *Angel* (The Women's Press, 1987) and *Rain Darling* (The Women's Press, 1990).

RHONDA COBHAM
AND MERLE COLLINS, EDITORS

WATCHERS AND SEEKERS

*CREATIVE WRITING BY BLACK WOMEN
IN BRITAIN*
Illustrated by Fyna Dowe

The Women's Press

First published by The Women's Press Limited 1987
A member of the Namara Group
34 Great Sutton Street, London EC1V 0DX
Reprinted, 1991

The editors would like to express their appreciation to Amryl Johnson
for allowing the title of her poem 'Watchers and Seekers' to be used
as the title of this collection.

British Library Cataloguing in Publication Data

Watchers and seekers : creative writing by
    black women.
    1. English literature—Women authors
    2. English literature—Black authors
    3. English literature—20th century
    I. Cobham, Rhonda   II. Collins, Merle
    820.8'09287   PR1110.W6

ISBN 0-7043-4024-0

Typeset by AKM Associates (UK) Ltd,
Ajmal House, Hayes Road, Southall, Greater London
Printed and bound in Great Britain by BPCC Hazell Books
Aylesbury, Bucks

The following poems have been previously published:

'Praise Song for My Mother' by Grace Nichols in *The Fat Black Woman's
Poems*, Virago Press, 1984; 'My Black Triangle' by Grace Nichols and 'For
Michael' by Valerie Bloom in *Angels of Fire*, ed. Sylvia Paskin, Jay Ramsay
and Jeremy Silver, Chatto and Windus, 1986; 'No More Fighting',
'Secret Woman', 'Strangers in a Hostile Landscape' and 'Disaster' by
Meiling Jin in *Gifts from my Grandmother*, Sheba, 1985; 'I Was That Woman'
by Debjani Chatterjee in the *Illustrated Weekly of India* in 1975; 'Dying in the
Street', 'Circle of Thorns' and 'like Dogs' by Amryl Johnson in *Early Poems
by Amryl Johnson*, Sable Publications, 1982.

A04949

820.92 C03

Contents

Foreword	1
Introduction	3
Woman Talk *by a-dZiko Simba*	13
Frailty Is Not My Name *by Maureen Ismay*	15
Surviving *by Maureen Ismay*	16
A Hankering After Truth *by Veronica Williams*	17
'She' *by Sista Roots*	19
One Angry Woman *by Veronica Williams*	21
Their Plan *by Sista Roots*	22
Images *by Merle Collins*	23
I Was That Woman *by Debjani Chatterjee*	27
My Black Triangle *by Grace Nichols*	29
Black Woman Out Dere *by Nefertiti Gayle*	30
Two Women I Know *by Rita Anyiam-St. John*	31
Same But Different *by Merle Collins*	32
No More Fighting *by Meiling Jin*	33
Don't Call Me Mama *by Carole Stewart*	34
Girl Talk *by Monique Griffiths*	36
Secret Woman *by Meiling Jin*	37
Hidden Reason *by Margot Jordan*	38
Illustration by Fyna Dowe	39
The Bed Sitting Room *by Maureen Ismay*	40
25.40 p.m. (past mourning) *by a-dZiko Simba*	50
No Say *by Millie Murray*	52
Ms Understood *by Sherma Springer*	54
I Wish You Had Warned Me *by Veronica Williams*	55
Nobody *by Brenda Agard*	56
I Love You It's True *by Carole Stewart*	58
How Times Have Changed! *by Merle Collins*	59
Jerry Perm Poem *by Carole Stewart*	61
For Me From You *by Rita Anyiam-St. John*	63
Even Tho *by Grace Nichols*	65
The Blue Flame *by Amryl Johnson*	66
Business Partners *by Brenda Agard*	68

One Man to Another *by Rita Anyiam-St. John*   70
Picture of a Woman *by Maureen Ismay*   71
Beloved *by Iyamide Hazeley*   72
Once *by Maud Sulter*   73
Illustration by Fyna Dowe   74
The Escape *by Millie Murray*   75
Mama *by Rita Anyiam-St. John*   83
The Inheritance *by Maureen Hawkins*   85
Where Are You My Bright-eyed Baby *by Maureen Ismay*   87
She Lives Between Back Home and Home
    by Sindamani Bridglal   88
A House *by Sandra Agard*   89
Nothing to Say *by Monique Griffiths*   95
Dying in the Street *by Amryl Johnson*   97
My Grandmother *by Maureen Ismay*   98
The Miracle *by Maureen Hawkins*   100
Praise Song for My Mother *by Grace Nichols*   101
Illustration by Fyna Dowe   102
Breaking Out of the Labels *by Leena Dhingra*   103
Pretty Girls Just Are *by Bunmi Ogunsiji*   108
Dictionary Black *by Sista Roots*   109
The Word *by Fyna Dowe*   111
Shipmates *by Merle Collins*   113
Beware of the Poison *by Hazel Williams*   115
Visual Conspiracy *by Fyna Dowe*   116
No Dialects Please *by Merle Collins*   118
Old Age Come to Us All *by Hazel Williams*   120
I Remember *by Rita Anyiam-St. John*   121
Strangers in a Hostile Landscape *by Meiling Jin*   123
i wondered *by Rita Anyiam-St. John*   127
'Silence is Nearer to Truth' *by Margot Jordan*   128
Babe *by Maud Sulter*   129
Illustration by Fyna Dowe   130
On Hurt *by Meiling Jin*   131
Nothing Said *by Brenda Agard*   132
Circle of Thorns *by Amryl Johnson*   133
Like Dogs *by Amryl Johnson*   134

Black Truth *by Brenda Agard* 136
De Youths *by Nefertiti Gayle* 138
Angry Children *by Carole Stewart* 140
Guess Who! *by Sista Roots* 142
Disaster *by Meiling Jin* 144
De Bubble Burs *by Fyna Dowe* 145
For Michael *by Valerie Bloom* 146
Life in Uncle Sam's Backyard *by Valerie Bloom* 148
Watchers and Seekers *by Amryl Johnson* 150
The Great Escape *by Sista Roots* 151
When You Have Emptied Our Calabashes
    by Iyamide Hazeley 152
Notes on the Contributors 154

Foreword

In recent years, there has been a marked increase in the volume of writing and performance by Black women in Britain.

This collection presents a selection of this work. Some of the writers are well known in Britain for the powerful presentation of their poetry at community and other events. Their work reflects the traditions of orature which are a powerful historical feature of Black creativity.

The images are of dreams, of visions, of hurt, of anger, of hope and of certainty of success in the struggle against oppression.

Introduction

> Sisterwoman sisterwoman
> Talk about the pleasure
> Talk about the pain (p. 13)

And across the decades a voice calls back, defiantly:

> I regret nothing –
> I have lived
> I have loved
> I have known laughter
> And dance and song,
> I have wept,
> I have sighed
> I have prayed,
> I have soared
> On fleecy clouds
> To the gates
> Of heaven,
> I have sunk
> Deep down
> In the pit of hell.[1]

In the search for foremothers to the writers presented in this anthology, the figure and work of the poet and playwright, Una Marson, cannot be overlooked. Marson died in 1965, before the creative writers presented here had started to write and, perhaps, before a few of them were born. Like them, however, she was a Black woman, determined to fashion her own definitions of both these concepts – Blackness and womanhood – through her art. In Jamaica, where Una Marson grew up and attended school, she quickly found herself on the outside of the social parameters of her world when, in her early poetry, she questioned the desirability of marriage as the ultimate goal of respectability for the Black middle-class woman. In England, where Marson lived as an adult and worked as personal secretary to the exiled Haile Selassie, as secretary of the League of Coloured People, and producer of the BBC programme, *Calling the Caribbean*, she acquired a new awareness of herself as a Black woman. This was at least in part a defensive reaction to the overt and covert racism of British society:

> I must not laugh too much,
> They say black folk can only laugh
> I must not weep too much,
> They say black folk weep always[2]

However, her new sense of a racial identity was equally the result of her affirmation of racial and cultural solidarity with the other Caribbean and African peoples among whom she worked in England. During this phase, Una Marson wrote poems celebrating the international women's movement; mourning poems for the Ethiopian soldiers who fell in the war against Mussolini; poems calling for Pan-African solidarity; and, in spite of the bloodthirsty mood of the years before the outbreak of World War II, poems in support of disarmament.

Back in Jamaica after the War, she plunged into new publishing and philanthropic ventures and attempted in her plays and poetry to build bridges back to the despised folk culture. Her poems experimenting with Jamaican Patwah and affirming a delight in Black beauty date from this period. Una Marson died, a middle-aged woman, from causes probably related to her frequent bouts of depression, or the punishing pace at which she lived and worked: both aspects of the price she had to pay for her insistence on creative freedom and an authentic sense of racial and sexual identity.

The writers whose works have been brought together in this anthology share with Marson an awareness of themselves, as Black people and as women, that informs their relationship to their art and their societies. Like her, many of them have lived between societies: Africa and the Caribbean; Africa and England; the Caribbean and England; India/Pakistan and England; China, the Caribbean and England. In terms of their womanhood and its implications at the level of personal relationships, they have a wider range of options than the choice between bourgeois marriage and spinsterhood which Marson could never quite accept (she remained single for most of her life but was ravaged by loneliness; married briefly near the end of her life but found neither security nor companionship). But though in today's world women can consider options which in Marson's age it would have been impossible to acknowledge, far less write about, the poems and short stories in this anthology remind us that the variety of alternatives does not make the choices any less painful:

> If you're black and on the game
> who can you really tell?
> Who wants to hear from a commodity
> that we never ever sell?
> And if you've had an abortion
> does even your best friend know?
> Or did you tell your boyfriend
> you had a particularly heavy flow? (p.36)

Where Marson's work wavers between stoic acceptance of solitude and the frustration caused by lack of sexual fulfilment, the writers here can tell of more painful forms of isolation, often experienced vicariously through the lives of their mothers:

> She waited
> till he got his shit together
> till he found himself

5

till he got a job
till he made it
and   she waited
and him sooon come
and she waited (p.50)

Una Marson's mother died while she was still at school. She herself never had children, although she was one of several gifted sisters who remained close to each other over the years. Her poems express a sense of having missed out on some of the most important emotional experiences available between women. Many of the writers whose work is included in this anthology explore the cycle of emotional and material inter-dependence between mother and daughter, grandmother and granddaughter, aunts and nieces, cousins, sisters, friends. Their perspectives may be critical, nostalgic or celebratory, senti-mental or distanced. But repeatedly there emerges a sense of sisterly solidarity with mother figures, whose strengths and frailty assume new significance for daughters now faced with the challenge of raising children and/or achieving artistic recognition in an environment hostile to the idea of female self-fulfilment:

I now know I must tell you
that sleep is now a slippery thing
daily eluding me, avoiding my every clutch
as boiling okro skips smoothly off the spoon

I am now
like mother like daughter
a regular rattler
me with pen and sheets of paper
you with scissors, machine and cloth (p. 84)

Such mothers, too, are our literary precursors: the would-be Black artists of a former generation who 'rattled', cooked and tended gardens but whose aesthetic achievement has been

6

buried in oblivion. Their influence remains in an instinct for style, a turn of phrase, a spontaneous gesture remembered dimly over generations. This is why Una Marson's significance for the writers in this volume goes further than the coincidence of race, gender and social situation. Marson was a pioneer for her time in the search for an authentic literary style: a style that could reflect and utilise the heritage of those half-forgotten voices, skills and gestures. Her search took her along many roads and up not a few blind alleys. She was, with her younger compatriot, Louise Bennett, one of the first women to use Jamaican Patwah in her poems as it was used by ordinary Jamaican women, at work and at prayer. But she also went a step further. In her poems on themes of Black female identity, she experimented with the borrowed rhythms of Afro-American Blues as a means of approaching issues which in her opinion had more than regional significance, or for which, as yet, she could locate no precedent in the Caribbean literary tradition:

> Gwine find a beauty shop
> Cause I ain't a lovely belle.
> The boys pass me by,
> They say I's not so swell.
>
> . . .
>
> I hate dat ironed hair
> And dat bleaching skin.
> Hate dat ironed hair
> And dat bleaching skin.
> But I'll be all alone
> If I don't fall in.[3]

There were other experiments – with the rhythms of Shakespeare and Kipling; with free verse and ballad rhyme schemes. Not all of them worked but Marson never broke faith with her conviction that a new consciousness demanded new techniques: a new voice that would somehow contain and explore the voices of past and present black communities.

When I came to read the comments the writers represented here made about their work and to listen to their reflections on the influences which had conditioned their styles, I was struck by the pattern of links which the writers themselves identified. The poetry and prose of Alice Walker and, to a lesser extent, the other Afro-American women writers now published in Britain were mentioned recurrently as a source of inspiration. Writers as different in temperament as the ebullient Millie Murray and the quietly perfectionist Maureen Ismay; as far flung as the Chinese/Guyanese Meiling Jin, living in London, and the Nigerian Rita Anyiam-St. John, working in Jos, mentioned the discovery of Afro-American women writers as a turning point in their creative development.

For writers like Grace Nichols, Merle Collins, Amryl Johnson and Valerie Bloom, whose formative years were spent in Guyana, Grenada, Trinidad and Jamaica respectively, there were definite links between their work and that of the established Caribbean writers who have experimented with Caribbean Creoles – Edward Brathwaite, Louise Bennett, Trinidad's Calypsonians and Jamaica's so-called 'Dub' poets. The insistent rhythms of the Reggae sound systems have also left their mark. Similarly the works of contributors like Fyna Dowe, Nefertiti Gayle and Sista Roots spring most vividly to life in oral performance.

The contributions from writers of Indian descent have been influenced by other cultural traditions. The plethora of imagery and crowded detail of a Hindu painting are suggested in Debjani Chatterjee's poetry. Gandhian contemplation and compassion set the tone in Leena Dhingra's essay, 'Breaking out of the Labels'. And yet, as Leena's essay reminds us, this access to Indian culture has been strengthened and given direction by the writers' understanding of themselves as part of a wider Black community. Perhaps this explains the similarity between Veronica Williams' crowded tapestries in 'One Angry Woman' and Debjani Chatterjee's 'I was that Woman'; or the absolute congruity of Sindamani Bridglal's evocation of the predicament of the Asian immigrant mother who 'lives between back home

8

and home'. We see her dilemma reflected in the experience of our mothers, our aunts, ourselves.

For writers who have grown up in Britain, Black music has been one of the most important sources of technical and rhythmic innovation. The Rock Steady sounds of childhood that Sandra Agard evokes in her prose poem, 'A House', have been joined in her work and that of writers like Brenda Agard, Margot Jordan, Bunmi Ogunsiji, Maureen Hawkins, Hazel Williams and a-dZiko Simba by the voices of Bob Marley, Joan Armatrading, Stevie Wonder, and old-time calypso. Listening to the way in which their 'Black British' speech rhythms were overlaid and complemented by Caribbean, Afro-American and, occasionally, African word patterns, I began to feel that the further the writers got from 'Home' the more responsive they seemed to become to the possibilities of interconnection between a range of Black voices that extended far beyond their immediate cultural experience.

The decision to include several short stories, an autobiographical essay and illustrations, in what was originally conceived of as a collection of poems, was our concession as editors to the exploratory pioneering nature of the work of these women. Maureen Ismay's haunting short story 'The Bed Sitting Room' seemed as much a poem as Sandra Agard's gently nostalgic 'A House' or Meiling Jin's political autobiography in verse 'Strangers in a Hostile Landscape'. Fyna Dowe's delicate line drawings set the mood for different sections of the anthology and add a subtle colouring to her creative profile which, after the militant tone of her poetry, may come as a quiet surprise. Fyna is not the only contributor for whom poetry is merely one of several media of creative expression. Brenda Agard's photography; Iyamide Hazeley's paintings and fashion design; Hazel Williams' skills as a choreographer; and the involvement of many of the women in theatre, publishing or radio, in spite of demanding academic programmes, the harsh realities of young motherhood in some cases, and recurrent spells of unemployment in others, were reminders for me of the strong traditions of independence and creativity that have

9

characterised Black female culture for hundreds of years.

This sense of a cultural tradition of survival is probably best seen in the poems on political themes and in the capacity for joyousness which often breaks through the works' most dismal scenarios. Some of the collection's most memorable lines were penned in response to specific social injustices. Here again, like Marson, the writers' larger sense of a Pan-African community, born out of the experience of exile, has made it easy for them to identify with political issues which go beyond their immediate realities. The fervour and poignancy with which Amryl Johnson and Brenda Agard register their outrage at the New Cross Massacre are matched by the sarcasm with which Sista Roots scourges those who profit from the South African apartheid system, and by Valerie Bloom's bitter caricature of 'Life in Uncle Sam's Backyard'. It is no accident that many of the images through which the writers express their sense of social outrage hark back to a shared history of exploitation through slavery.

> And
> I have seen
> I have seen
> I have seen
> I have seen the young willow
> sink beneath the waves
> beneath the waves
> beneath the hand which does not
> replenish (p.133)

But Black people do not weep always, and Black women do not spend their lives putting down men. Behind the sterner realities of their experiences, the writers in this volume have preserved laughter and a keen instinct for the absurd. One of my favourite poems in this collection is a short one by Carole Stewart that contains the impossible lines, 'But I love you and I loved Curly Wurlys/Mars bars and Fry's Turkish Delight./Now my sweet tooth is dead' (p.58). It connects with the irrepressible capacity for enjoyment that makes an adventure story out of family tragedy in Millie Murray's 'The Escape'. Then there's the ironic irreverence of Brenda Agard's 'Business Partners'; the openness to trust and love in Maud Sulter's 'Once'; the ability to bounce back in Margot Jordan's 'Hidden Reason' and 'Silence Is Nearer to Truth'; the note of steady optimism of Iyamide Hazeley's 'When You Have Emptied Our Calabashes' on which the collection closes. Add to that the intoxicating sensual power of Grace Nichols' poem 'My Black Triangle' and the sheer delight in sound of Fyna Dowe's 'De bubble still a bubble now de bubble burs'. Perhaps then you will understand why, each time I read through the collection, I have the illusion of being 'back home' for that family reunion of sisters and cousins we've been promising ourselves for years: where we'll cook home food, laugh raucously at the most inane jokes, share political obsessions and spiritual insights, rap about relationships and generally heal each other of all the scars of all those years of achieving and surviving like the strong Black women we cannot always be.

Rhonda Cobham
Bayreuth 1986

1 Una Marson, 'Confession,' *Heights and Depths*, Kingston, The Gleanor Co., 1937.
2 'Black Burden,' *Towards the Stars*, Bickley, University of London Press, 1945.
3 'Kinky Hair Blues,' *The Moth and the Star*, Kingston, The Gleanor Co., 1937.

Woman Talk

Sisterwoman sisterwoman
Talk about the pleasure
Talk about the pain

Don't save up your emotion
for a stormy day
Don't let pent-up anger reign
rain, reign, rain, reign, rain
down
on the ones you love

Take that feeling
don't fake that feeling
    make that feeling your own

Sisterwoman sisterwoman
Talk about the pleasure
Talk about the pain

Don't hide your feelings behind blank eyes
(a thin disguise for your hurt)
Don't cry
behind closed doors
Don't try
to smother the sobbin
the sobbin, the sobbin, the sobbin, the sobbin,
the sobbin and the heavin
of a million tear-filled moments
strangled into silence.

Take that feeling
don't fake that feeling
    make that feeling your own

Sisterwoman sisterwoman
Talk about the pleasure
Talk about the pain

and when joy and laughter
overwhelms you
and threatens to split you
from head to toe
let them know
Throw back your head
open your mouth
and laugh
    laugh
    LAUGH
    OUT
    LOUD
let the highest leaf on the tallest tree
let the smallest ant in the deepest valley
    dance
    to the rhythms of your fun
Take that feeling
Don't fake that feeling
    make that feeling your own

Sisterwoman sisterwoman
Talk about the pleasure
Talk about the pain

and sisterwoman know yourself
and sisterwoman feel yourself
and sisterwoman be yourself

and

Sisterwoman

find peace

a-dZiko Simba

14

Frailty Is Not My Name

Frailty is not my name
                 yet,
On the other hand,
I'm not a big strong, black woman
iron hard and carrying
all the sorrows of the world on my back.

My breasts large and hard as boxes
My eyes big and bulging
My skin, black and shiny and greasy

I'm not big and strong
and keeping a man underneath my tail
able to take all that garbage
                'Here dawg take that'

        I'm no mythology
        shaking the earth
        and freaking out the leaves.

I'm not a strong black woman
admirable and brawd

ten children at my breast
all at the same time
while cooking and cleaning
and singing and fixing up
my man . . .
with beads in my hair
and camel on my skin.

On the other hand
        Don't call me frailty!

Maureen Ismay

Surviving

Surviving
Just surviving
Keeping it all at bay
and just having enough to pay
just enough to eat
just surviving on the little pay
and sending the kids to school
Where will the money come from?

Just surviving
an yu cyaan see thru yu yeye
fa yu just surviving . . .
on the little
when you haven't any strength
left in you body –
just surviving

Dem a seh you lazy
when yu jus surviving
on the little
Dem seh dis
an dem seh dat
when yu jus surviving
when they take more than they give
And yu sick
yu sick so
and struggling, struggling
Just surviving . . .

Maureen Ismay

A Hankering After Truth

I'd look back and see the coffee mornings,
Dinner parties, picnics on the lawn
Late night guitar playing in the bedsit,
Weekends in Paris living on watermelons;
Punting down the Thames,
Listening to Moustaki lyrics on the record player
And thinking about illusive truth,
Illusive, ill, loose, lucid.

The children have taken over my life
Temporarily;
They have become wholly absorbing,
The baby one more so than the older.
Babies are like that.
I become like them, lost in a world of make belief.

People have complained lately
That it's difficult to get close.
I put up barriers and I know it.
It must be due to disappointments,
Or the shortcomings of men,
Or too-high expectations.
If only I could go back to the years before they were born
And recapture the then me,
I'd see a world where people made an impression
On my consciousness
that kept me alive and responsive,
Because they hankered after truth.
Truth
Illusive truth;
Illusive, ill, loose, lucid.

The young Oxford student who drank more than was
    good for him.
Who watched his father slowly die of cancer;
Who missed too many tutorials because

he was reading me his poems
And thrashing out the meaning of life.
His father was a doctor who could not say
Physician
heal thyself!

Another young man
Who showed me one of his poems.
It had six lines
Six words in each line
And all the words were the same.
They started with F!
I burst out laughing, surprised.
'You'll never publish that,' I said.
He sunk closer down on the lounge.
'You know,' he said,
I always get these feelings when I'm with you.'
I wasn't sure what he meant;
was he talking about inspiration.
'No, I mean, I get these feelings, but when I
Get here, they're completely gone.'
I didn't know how to take that,
Whether as a compliment
Or a sign of an innate unattractiveness.
I was reassured;
'You have a purity of soul,' he said.

They were always young men,
Searching after truth,
Illusive truth,
Illusive, ill, loose, lucid.

Veronica Williams

'She'

Born a girl child
Into this world
    Wild
Appearing as a flower
More beautiful
By the hour
Mummy's little pearl
And Daddy's little girl

Forwarding bolder
As she gets older
Learning the tricks
Flashing her eyes
With surprise
No more toys
Attention on boys
And false love's Joys

Time has flown
Now she's full grown
Colour telly
Big belly
She's feeling sick
'im fly her two lick

She choke up
    Inside
She ain't
    His bride
She ain't
    His wife
Let's look at her life

Worryin' 'bout
That speck of dust
Clean it
Or he'll make

A fuss

Wash the clothes
Cook the food
Hurry or else
He'll be in a mood

Never has time
To think
For herself
Priority being
What's cheap
On the shelf

On the bed
With one eye shut
Trying to avoid
That pain
In her gut

Just as she fall
The baby start bawl
She cover her ears
And fight back
The tears

Shut in a box
Did she
Iron his socks

Just like
She granny
And she mother
        Unlike
She father
And she brother

This can't be life
There must be another!

Sista Roots

One Angry Woman

I am a woman and I'm angry
With a world that pigeon-holed me
Into stereotyped roles I do not fit into.
I am angry at the shortsightedness
That sees not male and female as persons merely.
Marriage does not interest me and the nuclear family
Feeds in on itself.
It's claustrophobic.
I'd like to breathe.
Men only interest me if
They have more than a bag of sperms to identify them;
These days,
You can get that in a bank!
But a man's mind, ah, that's something
Quite different.

I am a woman and I'm angry
At having to behave in ways female.
I'd like to climb rocks and build a bridge
To shoot the menstrual cycle up in a spaceship.
But I'd like to be pampered after building
With long slim glasses of cherried liqueur
Under starlit, moonbeamed nights
And have a man from every country in the world
Dancing to my every need,
And look on this as my right!

I am a woman and I'm angry.
I have a brain and I'd like to use it
To fill the world with beautiful images
Real and imagined.

Veronica Williams

Their Plan

Who says
  I should wear a skirt

Who says
  The Earth is dirt

Who says
  I should look like you

Who says
  I should do as you do

Who says
  It's time to eat

Who says
  I should eat meat

Who says
  I should comb my hair

Who says
  The best is 'fair'

I am
  What I am
I'll do what
  I can
to destroy
  Their plan

Sista Roots

Images

The mind remembers
images it met from birth
images that marked out margins
before I knew of words
of meaning
faces ever present
faces mostly absent
images that came to splinter pain
forbidden shouts
forbidden search
images created in other people's
mind–lessness

Images wrapped in skin-tight words
like
Woman
weak as straw
coward as fly
devious as Delilah
hammer-blows
upon the distant ever-present self
like

Dat boy fou fou eh
He really stupid
Just like a girl
And you know . . .
I laughed
And laughed again at
Dat person in front o me
drivin like a real bebe
ah sure is a blasted woman
But
Woy!
You don't see dat girl
how she handle dat car so beautiful!

She good boy!
Just like a man!

The message
Subdue your excellence
if you want to keep your identity
as woman
walk within the patterns I shape
after my image
within my likeness

images
battering the receptive everforming mind
watching women watching children
women watching houses
his house
registered in his name
of course
your labour – for love
and gratitude for his presence
his labour – for wealth
and you, a peaceful person
would be quietly violated
would not make the demands
that make revolutions
you, a peaceful person
would keep your weakness
and cherish your chains

images
watching women
labour without value
working all day
working no place
working women
quietly asking at end of week
for another twenty dollars plea-a-a-se
to buy shoes for Jim

working women biting lips
as he sucks his teeth
biting back words forming blood
at the corners of her cheeks

images of our anger
images of our shouts
why don't you fight back
Hush chile
sometimes you have to play dead
To see what funeral you go get
so accustomed to the game
that even after the funeral over
we still playin dead

lookin wise
talkin wise
actin stupid
mind touching tender distances
going through the movements
according to the script
not realising perhaps
that whatever the struggle
until we make it different
the boss will always win
the boss will always register in his name
the sweat
the blood
the tears
of workers
till workers claim their worth

reshaping meaning
reshaping values
reshaping language
reshaping caring
working towards the vision
of a sharing beauty

reality that we will create
if only
only if
we insist on equal worth.

Merle Collins

I Was That Woman

At the very beginning of creation
I was dormant, potential, Pandora's box,
A package deal for Adam,
A surprise birthday present
With a time-bomb ticking inside.
He opened me with wonder,
He tasted me with delight.
I was that woman, ashamed and resentful,
Wise yet weak, bold but blushing,
With lowered eyes I walked away from Eden
Without a backward glance, smouldering.
The first rebel, I was the mother of Cain,
And was punished with pain and servitude.
I was that woman, pure and radiant,
Abducted by a demon across the sea;
Banished but dutiful, I bore twin kings,
Till exhausted at last I cried for the earth.
I was that woman outraged by a hundred;
My modesty a never-ending sari,
While righteous husbands watched in silence,
The handling of their property, the strangling of their pride.
I was the woman of mystery and magic
Who sang on the waves and waved my wand
To provide adventures for heroic men on an obstacle course.
I was that beautiful horror with snake-hair
To be slain with a shudder by the brave.
My crime is that I felt for a fellow victim,
Woman-like I wept for fallen Lucifer.
I was that woman, poor and lowly,
Who hid behind a tree and offered
My single garment to the mendicant sage.
I was that woman who tearfully pleaded
And pestered the Compassionate One
To relent and admit me and my kind.
I was that woman who bowed and listened

To Mahavir's message of hope: release
Is mine in a next life – as a man.
I was that woman who destroyed my breast
To fight with men on their own ground.
I was that woman of ill repute
Who washed those feet with repentant tears,
Grateful that he would not lift a stone;
But accepting my untouchable lot.
I was that woman trapped in a brothel,
Who cared not for heaven or hell,
But loved Allah in spite of his masculinity.
I was that woman who roused a nation
And was burnt so many times at so many stakes.
I was the woman at whom the Vedas, the Avesta,
The Bible and the Koran were flung;
Their God was the bogeyman
Who kindly sent male prophets
To keep me humble in my place.
I was that woman, silly and rouged,
Of endless chatter, and timeless in dressing,
Whose mind is full-blown and scattered with the wind,
Whose moods mysterious like the tides
Fluctuate with the changing moon.
I was that woman whose nude body inspired
While the sculptor appreciated and chiselled.
I was the woman with soul desecrated
Who typed away from ten to five with two tea–breaks.
I was that woman at the helm of six hundred million,
Who longed to be accepted as simply human:
A real person like others, and not a myth.
I was the woman, neurotic, torn, disowning my sex.
I was the voluptuous, decorative, drudge;
I was the creature with will power raped.
I was that woman . . .

Debjani Chatterjee

28

My Black Triangle

My black triangle
sandwiched between the geography of my thighs

is a bermuda
of tiny atoms
forever seizing
and releasing
the world

My black triangle
is so rich
that it flows over
on to the dry crotch
of the world

My black triangle
is black light
sitting on the threshold
of the world

overlooking my deep-pink
probabilities

and though
it spares a thought
for history
my black triangle
has spread beyond his story
beyond the dry fears of parch-ri-archy

spreading and growing
trusting and flowing
my black triangle
carries the seal of approval
of my deepest self

Grace Nichols

Black Woman Out Dere

Black woman out dere have no fear
Fight back my sisters, Fight back.

An if you struggle is you fat
An you man pon you back,
An him say you too fat
Fight back my sisters, Fight back.

Black woman out dere, dem say
You gaan mad, dem wan put
You inna mad house, true you
depress an sad de pressure so
Hard . . .
When you man lef de yard,
You pickney in need an want
little feed
Fight back my sista, Fight back.

An you want little wuk and you
Can't get no wuk, all you can get . . .
Is de white man dut, so you resort
to crime to earn a dime an you en up on street a walk
frontline, an de man on dere jus a watch you behin.
Fight back Black sista, Fight back.

Black woman out dere wid troubles an fears,
Dem say you livin in sin
Cause you livin's thin an you givin away
A little sin ting.
You na beg no body no golden ring.
You only wan fe earn you own ting.
Fight back Black sistas, Fight back.

Black woman out dere you have to Fight back,
Jus come forward wid a double attack,
No boder weep
On no kitchen mat . . . Jus Attack.

Nefertiti Gayle

Two Women I Know

The two women I know
one lies on the sunbed thing
soaking in rays of light
one dreads the sun like plague
rubbing in jars of bleaching cream
these women that I know
one wants what the other has
the other what the other's got.

I know for I know them both
when any terminates her ordeal
I know for each comes to me
right hand placed beside my left
or left beside my right.
At the different times I see them
hand beside my own
one says,
'Right? I'm getting there
Can't wait to get there
I'll be quite chic soon enough.'
The other says,
'The thing dey work o
I don dey yellow
I don dey yellow pass you
small time now
I go be proper sissy, abi?'

All I do is shake my head
for I don't know what to say
for one her sunbed with its glaring
rays dazzles me no end
for the other
her jars and jars
of bleaching and fading creams
and these endless jars
jar me endlessly.   *Rita Anyiam-St. John*

Same But Different

My friend and I
travelled home together by night bus
My friend is white
As we parted at the station-stop
she said
that her fears
were of rapists and robbers
for me
that too
But as I walked the distance home
on pounding tiptoe
Each sudden shadow
was a threat of the National Front

Merle Collins

No More Fighting

I can't fight with you sister, any more.
I will talk with you
And share the pain
But I won't fight with you.

We argue
And shout
We beat each other on the breast
All the time.
And we're so busy
We don't notice
Gwei lo*
Come and take
Our children away.

I will not fight with you sister, any more
For the road's too long and hard
And I need all my strength
To stay on it.

Meiling Jin

* white ghost

Don't Call Me Mama

Don't call me Mama
Don't call me Mother
See me for what I am
A Woman.

Even though you crawled
I pushed you out from under me.
I teased you with my breast.
It gave me pain
It gave me pleasure
It gave you life.

Don't call me Mama
A stalwart of the nation.
Don't call me Mother
The backbone of the struggle.
See me here for what I am
A Woman.

Throughout our history
You call me Mother.
You ban your belly
And call me Mama.
How much longer?
Will you learn?
My Motherhood is not my Womanhood
Just another dimension
of me
A Woman.

I am here in the struggle
I am here – part of the nation
I am here in Afrika
I am here in Britain
I am here in the Caribbean
I am here in the Americas
I am here on the Frontline

A Woman.

Mama, Mother
A sign of respect.
When you call me Mama
Do you see my Woman?
When you struggle for sustenance
between my breasts,
Call me Mother, Tower of Strength,
Keeper of Tradition
Do you see my Woman?

Before my belly bloated with another life,
My teeth clenched
and the sweat of labour
burnt my eyes
I was Woman.
Before you called me
Before you whispered 'Mother'
Before you cried out 'Mama'
I was Woman.

When you mourn my passing
Mourn my Woman.
Don't call me Mama
Don't call me Mother
See me for what I am
A Woman.

Carole Stewart

Girl Talk

Cha, me tired of men whistling at me
when I walking the government street.
And why the knowing glances and stares
when our eyes accidentally meet?
I'm fed up of being furtively fondled
without my knowledge or consent.
Wonder if those loving words
were contrived or lovingly meant?
If you're black and on the game
who can you really tell?
Who wants to hear from a commodity
that we never ever sell?
And if you've had an abortion
does even your best friend know?
Or did you tell your boyfriend
you had a particularly heavy flow?
God, when I start to think of it
I feel my head gon bus
We must write it all down
cos is who we can really cuss?
Black child, be strong out there
Cos sometimes you can't let it out
but the rest of us keeping silent
we still know what ya talking bout.

Monique Griffiths

Secret Woman

Are you the woman
i dreamt one night:
came to my house,
spoke with me,
into whose eyes i gazed,
and between us passed,
something,
i'm not sure what?

Or was it someone else i dreamt?
Or am i dreaming now,
of a strange, secret woman?

Like ships in the night:
a temporary respite
from this loneliness.
On the fringes of
i and i

A question of mistake
i did not feel your hand
softly stroking my back,
or your eyes,
gazing into mine.

i only dreamt your tenderness
as i lay asleep one night
waking
dreaming
wishing.

Meiling Jin

Hidden Reason

My reason which was once severed,
Cut into unconscious divisions,
Hidden in maladroit madness;
Is now returning with a bounce
Welcoming the spring's green trees
Which promise a new soundness of mind
And a new beginning from the little I have left.

Margot Jordan

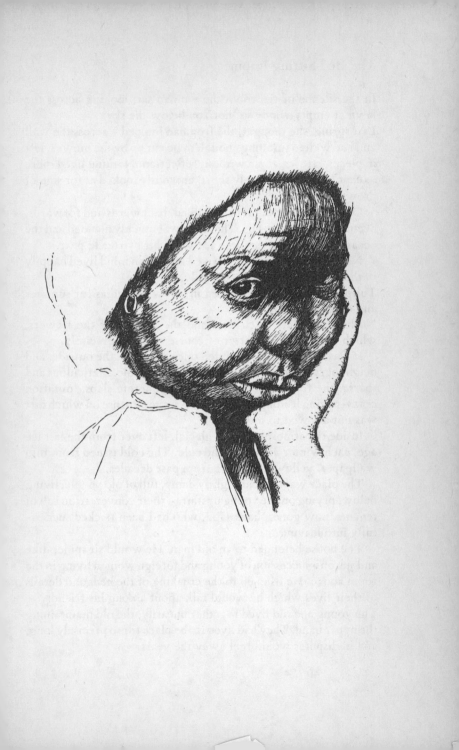

The Bed Sitting Room

In the silence of the room the woman sat, looking across the lawn at empty windows, horizon below the sky.

Last spring, she thought, the frog had jumped – across the wall and had waited just long enough to be cut up by the mower, left in pieces, strewn, done without reflection. Nothing lived there except grass cut precisely short, anxiously looked at for sign of growth.

Occasionally at night cats walked, backwards and forwards, eventually leaving trails. The fence was quickly mended and the occasional cat that ventured forward, hit by sterile pear.

Nothing that was not contrived by human mind lived happily in the garden. Even then, uneasily.

Tulips for springtime, planted in a row, begonias for summer and crocuses in autumn.

Nothing was left to chance, and the colours of the flowers, which bloomed as a matter of course, glowed precisely.

It was an old house – painted once a year on the outside, and neighbours could not say it was not respectable. Meticulous and sparse, the front covered with large concrete slabs, imitation crazy-paving leading to the door. A large expanse on which dirt was not allowed to settle.

Inside the atmosphere was glacial, left over from the last ice age, each winter adding to the cold. The cold issued from thin wallpaper, yellow and white from past decades.

The place was old and slightly damp, full of old people, living below, prying on the young upstairs – their conversation full of tenants, now gone, thank God, who had been tricked successfully into leaving.

The house belonged to an old man. He would sit spider-like and spy on a succession of young and foreign women living in the room above. He listened to the creaking of the beds and details of their lives which he would talk about among his friends.

The young and old lived together uneasily, the old maintaining the upper hand. They had lived in the place for so precisely long, and in disputes would reel away the years.

The right to live exactly as they pleased; the right to use the line; to complain about the movement of the people above, etc. It was three to two and from the start unfair. The two young people living above were constantly reminded of the rights which they did not have.

The young people came and went in quick succession, mostly women who could find nowhere else to go. Foreign women, defenceless, they would see, pinned on notice boards, tucked away in corridors:

A nice room in respectable
establishment. Vacant.
                    Apply
                    Mr Wint.

They would be told how near it was to transportation, a hint of peace and freedom, lured long enough for agreements to be signed.

The woman came one spring day not intending to stay, it was necessity which drove her there. The hard wallpaper, the narrow room in which the outstretched hand touched the wall was slightly repellent, but tolerable in comparison to others she had seen. Places with corridors smeared with grease. Long corridors smelling of unwashed people. Bathless places.
She had been worn out by the endless futile search.
Felt like leaving notices in windows saying:

Nice girl needs place to live.
Anything will do.
No boyfriends, cats, or dogs.

Then she would appear on doorsteps. Suspicious eyes peer out, doors slam in her face.

I'm a nice girl, she thought. no boyfriends and no dogs. But perhaps that was the reason – she did not have a man. She remembered long ago – at sixteen, leaving home – her mother had screamed after her, 'Where is the man – let me see him!'

41

She had been bewildered, retreated quickly, puzzled by her mother's words – the only reason a girl should leave home was to set up house, with a man.

She had lived at first with a man, a wife and another lodger. Living on tinned soups and sandwiches from the corner shop, surviving as best she could.

Slowly the wife had begun to encroach on her life, entering the room, searching – perhaps to find the husband secreted in a cupboard ... or sandwiched in between the bed. She would turn the bed over and look closely, each week. A young girl alone ... better to be safe than sorry. She could never trust her man, bred in her by long tradition – a man should never be trusted especially with a younger woman, unattached.

Eventually, one night, after the rent was paid, they popped the question: 'Where is the Mr?' they said together, smiling, as if it was something they had thought out carefully, but indelicate to ask directly. 'There is no one,' the girl had replied, not quite sure ...

'A pretty girl like you ... etc.' She was lacking in something essential to a pretty girl and was defective, she did not have that one vital accessory which would have acted like a crossed 't' or a final dot.

The woman eyed her with scorn. Passing in corridors she would hear a cackle at her back ...

The man eyed her with speculation and winks ...

In summer she walked by dank riverbanks alone, suffering pollen, and quickly ran up the stairs when it was time to go to bed. She was lacking in essentials.

She knew she would not find a place to live because, on opening the door, they would see an empty space where the essential accessory should stand. They would smile, allow her to see the room, but ask, 'Where ...?' They would also say, 'We have other people coming – two girls sharing ...' They would think, on seeing her alone ...

'Is she on the game? Is she a ...?

Why is she alone?'

They would smile and say, 'Come in' while eyeing her with

suspicion . . . looking at her shoes: 'I can always tell a person by the shoes they wear – I used to like B — until she changed her shoes.'

'Is she a tart, is she queer?' they would ask themselves. The price of my shoes fixes the rest of me . . . But if you are poor well . . . 'You will never catch a man that way, luv, not with them shoes.' Is she a tart . . .? Is she queer . . .? The woman looked at her shoes – worn out by now. She realised that she could find a convenient chauffeur to drive her from place to place to disarm landladies and reassure . . . that the rent would be paid. He would only ask a small price for his solicitations – a simple matter of sex – and after all it was only giving and receiving.

Perhaps she should pretend and drop references to a presence: 'My B says . . . My B likes . . . My B . . . My B . . .' constantly filling every space with My B.

After all, a girl cannot do without a mister . . .

Once, long ago, someone had explained the facts of life and on ending said, 'So you see, dear, you cannot do without a man.'

Or practical grandmotherly advice: 'Mary – yu ha fe wuk; yu ha fe support yuself, but yu need a man to warm the bed at night. Let dem marr'ed all dem like, but yu ha fe wuk an support yuself, dat is all a aax, fi yu me only grandaater. Yu no want no man to push yu roun.'

She had complained to her mother about the worn-out shoes, fatigue and loneliness, had been told:

'Get yuself a nice likkle car an a television set!'

Worlds – unreconcilable.

She thought of catching man, ending it all, to retire to the kitchen to 'cook his dinner'.

She also thought of the humiliation . . . of asking for the rent, a new dress, a pair of knickers . . .

Once, in the market place, a man stood, with his wife behind, in front of a stall selling underwear for women. He stood territorially, his wife behind, her head covered. 'How much is that?' he demanded, reaching forward to inspect. His wife behind him said, her voice thin and slight, 'But . . .' She was ignored. He continued to inspect and finally decided, 'It would not fit.' Loudly proclaimed: 'I am the only person to get inside this. It must fit.'

Eventually he walked away, his wife following behind.

The woman continued to walk the streets, until finally one day, she had found the place.

It was furnished well and cheaply, with a single bed. There was only room to sit before the fire.

She did not intend to stay, growing mouldy with the old. Instead, she thought of all there was to do. Her life lay an uncut dress. She would make designs and become famous in large fashion houses, travel the world, discover pasts obscured by blunted words. She looked in the white mirror and saw herself staring back like a photograph, slightly unreal, and wondered why she was tinged with green, her face copper brown instead of smooth and dark.

Initially her friends had come to see her there and, met with grumbles from the old, had soon departed and did not return.

She thought of doing something significant with her life instead of marrying. Planned her life to this end. Carefully dressing each day, she would first make a series of telephone calls, keeping in contact . . . and gathering a portfolio of designs, she would tour the city. Allowed potbellied men, more interested in her looks, to finger her work, shaking heads and passing her on. One old man informed her, 'It's not bad – but you need to make compromises – to be a little generous . . .' His words trailed away . . .

She walked the city until one day she hid her life, herself, her work, her identity under the bed – never to be ressurrected.

To recoil into disillusion and depression.

Her dreams had ended. She would grow old in the house, living there forever.

The house was deathly quiet, yellow paint and cracks flaking. Rails ran effortlessly from the top of the stairs to the bottom. Bars in between regularly spaced. Dirt lay in patches on the linoleum.

Occasionally, on complaint, the landlord would replace a small piece of carpet for another duller and cheaper.

Even in summer the air hung limp and cold.

The woman sat alone, staring at the orange and white wallpaper which assaulted from the wall.

In winter little light came through the window, skated over the bottom of the bed, disappearing into the carpet.

She crouched around the fire while the wind blew up her skirt, and hoped the landlord would come and mend the window. Instead, collecting rent, he would lecture on 'the correct way of living simply', boasting of his frugality.

He outlined his breakfast, dinner and tea. He ate nothing but yoghurt, vinegar, and honey. He was healthy for his years.

One day passing on the stairs the smell of cooking meat drifted from the cracks in his door . . .

While he talked her gaze wandered to the lump at the top of his head, gleaming, like a piece of brain which had wandered out of place.

He had been to India, fed the poor, walked the streets of Bombay and pressed money into the hands of beggars. He had dispensed charity to the world and like a banker expected returns. He had no sympathy for the urban poor near to home.

The woman was alone and poor.

He collected the rent each month, bending slightly to peer at paper notes. Counting one by one with nervous fingers. He ignored pleading voices that said, 'There is a draught . . .' Instead, fingering the notes, would leave, smiling slightly. He had won again with little effort.

He had worked the city and known ways of taking without giving in return. Frustrated with retirement, he plied his skills on women without defences.

The city still remained in his posture, his tensed-up shoulders and scattered teeth.

When finally cornered, he pleaded ignorance and posturing baboon-like – screech loudly – so that all would know his innocence, and demolish with personal abuse.

She felt withered away among the scheming, withered people, the gossips and antiseptic medical students who came and went in extraordinary succession.

Perhaps she would end her days lingering on street corners, wrapped in newspapers, bruised and battered, frost cold, abused, thrown out like refuse under arches to die. Nobody's grandmother, or children taken away at birth to be brought up by strangers, forever mourned, forever unknown.

Perhaps a woman old and sterile among gossips, days passing in trivia, extemporating on trivia, to conceal the yawning gap that says there is nothing there. Nothing had been left because there was nothing there before. Where life had been allowed to drift by, day after day after day. An old woman wrapped in blankets, crouched on feeble fire saying, 'At least I have worked, contributed to the killing, I am entitled to sit still.' An old woman who nobody goes to see, for in truth she had given her fingers, now arthritic, and had lost her brain in wars and in the service of a man. Now instead she pries on unwitting tenants – young women – defending her territory, the men in her house.

The house was rather dirty.

Sometimes the woman walked up and down on creaking floorboards to emphasise her anger at the damp and perhaps express her torture to the old man listening downstairs. She felt like running away from prison bars, the yellow walls which assumed proportions of torture – yellow flakes falling on her head on opening the door, yellow psychedelic patterns reaching out to suck her in, at morning time. It seemed as if only in sleep could she escape the room. Sometimes she dreamed of yellow hospital beds and old women coughing lives away, and on opening her eyes would see yellow and cover her face with yellow. Yellow summers faded into yellow autumn.

The winter smells of the house were almost suffocating. Drowned in rancid clothes, unwashed dogs and breathing people. Sprays from sweet-smelling canisters floated in climatic zones. At the bottom of the stairs individual grains hung, almost visible, in the air. At the top, thick smells – old lamb and dead dogs. Leering smells, assaulting.

She had lived in tiny rooms, it seemed, forever – and there was no chance of escape. She would shrivel, old among the old, imprisoned. Mind trapped in decaying body, exterminated.

After all she was a black, and it was the habit of the old woman to routinely remove, as one removing weeds, the blacks: 'Filthy things, eating food and making the noise they call music.' She would gather all her ingenuity and expel, listening at keyholes until she had found a formula and then would strike at unwary victims who felt sorry for old English women, not knowing that her only pleasure left was 'getting rid of blacks'. Afterwards she would boast and gloat – another job well done.

The young black woman, for now she had been harried into awareness of self against the pale and rotting flesh, was caged; aware of the machinations of people like animals living in sterile jungles.

She felt abused, spied on by old men who peeped through keyholes when she bathed: she would hear the creaking of the floorboards and the tapping of feet running away quickly; hear breathing and catch a glimpse of pale and sagging body disappearing behind a door.

Sometimes angered, she would scream when emerging from the loo, would see, at precisely the right moment, one naked body flashing, standing still, in front of her. She screamed at the calculation, the precision in timing of the deaf old man, between the flushing of the loo and her emergence. She felt like hitting hard, or cutting off offending organ paraded before her every morning, like a ritual.

Later on, meeting in the streets, he would poke his tongue out and roll it around his lips obscenely.

She risked her life in the traffic.

Even escaping to the park, to breathe fresh air, she would come across an old man among waterbirds, and fleeing would see a yellow car, an old man watching.

The landscape became an old man dank and silent, watching, poking out his tongue.

It seemed that she could never escape from old men. Once on coming to mend a broken hinge, the landlord, an old man, pressed close against her, breathing heavily, the smell of unwashed dogs. It was as if they thought, 'Young women alone should always be abused.'

Her mind began to drip away, and like a prison she began only to see the walls around her pressing. Outside blanketed, vestigial. She began to go outside only in the evening so that spying eyes from curtains would not watch her movements. She sat and shivered in the damp and cold in the middle of summer; could hear echoes of children playing in the distance, next door but far away. Her mind became an empty space, left for illusion to gather. There was nothing left but old and dying people.

Once someone had said, 'When there is nothing left, a girl can always marry.'

She began to wonder about the women who had lived there, in the room before her. She had heard of women leaving to have babies. Women who left evidence of their passing. Wrapping paper and soft synthetic toys lying at the bottom of drawers. Smells of cheap perfumes had lingered on the air, speaking volumes of babies and boyfriends waiting in the wings.

The woman walked through the streets at evening time, windblown and lonely, aware of isolation. Desolation delineated by falling autumn leaves, yellow and red. Grey slated sky like roofs hanging from above.

Dogs' messes lay drying. Wind blew leaves, eddying carefree along the road. She saw branches which reminded her of bars and which stood in her way, to be pried apart.

In the distance she saw a walking figure, coming closer, to be

48

identified. The landlord, thin and slightly bent. She spoke, saying 'Hello' out of courtesy. His eyes suddenly assumed a lost and vacant look as if, having nowhere to look, he had turned inwards. It had happened before, and over the years she had come to realise that he would never speak to her in the streets. She did not exist, in spite of the paid rent every month, in spite of the body pressed close, inside the intimacy of her room.

It was time to go. By now grown cynical, she wondered if this charade would not play itself again and again and again! Without a mister.

She walked to the centre of town, caught a lift, went up almost into the sky and walked to the white edge.

On one grey day.

She paused for one moment looking down – into the vacuum below.

Behind her, life had slipped into empty spaces, grey landscape . . . surrounding.

The winter wind dashed across her face – she moved away.

She could not pick up pieces shattered on the walls, could not turn back into vacancy . . .

The lines in her hands ran like madness, broken like the years.

Silence and the winter winds.

Maureen Ismay

25.40 p.m. (past mourning)

twenty five
and she waited
and him sooon come
and she waited

she waited
till he bought a draw
till he checked a spar
till he did some runnings
till he looked up an ex-girl friend
and she waited
and him sooon come
and she waited

she waited
till he got his shit together
till he found himself
till he got a job
till he made it
and   she waited
and him sooon come
and she waited

she waited
in her party clothes
outside supermarkets with shopping bags full
lying in that big empty bed
groaning in hospital holding her fat belly
and   she   waited
and him sooon come
andshewaited

she waited
for dreams to come true
for the phone to ring
for the door to knock
for a sign

and   she   waited
and him sooon come
and she waited

she waited
in darkened rooms
hating her reflection
eating herself silly
drinking herself blind
AND SHE WAITED
and him sooon come
and

                              she waited

Until one day
she looked at her watch
fifteen years had gone by
could it be   she was running fast?
(or maybe *he* was running slow)
Either way she had waited long enough
The Waiting Game was no more fun
She picked up herself
                         and walked out the door
She was forty
              and her life had just begun

                    a-dZiko Simba

No Say

(To be performed using three voices)

He says what and what I have to do – to be – to live
He doesn't even listen to me – I must do what
He says
He says I'm wasting my time wanting to be a ballerina
He says there's no future in it for any Black girl
He says   I'm to be a nurse
He says   That's all Black girls are good for.
He says   I must come out him house – if me nor gwan listen!
He says   I day dream too much – But that's all I can do
              I dream of being Odette in *Swan Lake*
He says   I'm too fool for anything
He says   He's my father   I come under his rule.

He says   'Me never bin with a gal so black'
He says   He likes nurses though
He says   I should feel lucky to be with him considering he
              can have any girl
              light skin–red skin–white skin–indian hair
He says   I can't even grind my hips
He says   He's wasting his time
              I think I love him, so I hold on to him.
He says   'It's time me breed yu'
              I can't stand the pain
He says   'Yu lucky it's a boy pickney or me woulda gone '
He says   He's my man

He says   He's hungry – haven't I cooked yet
He says   If I've ironed his clothes he's going out
He says   How can I tell him what time to come home
He says   His white friends don't have hassles at home
He says   He's tired of hearing my voice
              I tried to please him only he doesn't realise
He says   Why get a Saturday job – I'm there to keep him
He says   Just because I've wasted my life – Don't blame him

        Pain can't bear   No escape
He says   He can understand why his father left
He says   He's my son – Not a senseless object

He says – He says – He says   I say – Nothing

Millie Murray

Ms Understood

She may not understand why it is that
her opinion is found to be irrational
her point of view insignificant
her feelings ignored
her logic illogical
her facts inaccurate
why her actions are inclined to be of no importance.

She may not understand why it is that
her suspicions are unfounded
her reasoning unreasonable
her beliefs unbelievable
her intelligence underestimated
her authority undermined
why her meaning is never understood.

She cannot understand why it is that he can do no wrong

But she can understand why it is that
she is unhappy.

Sherma Springer

54

I Wish You Had Warned Me

I wish you had put a red light on
To warn me of the mystery behind closed doors.
I'd always felt free to walk in
Uninvited.

I wish you had said something –
Given a hint of the ensuing danger
That was to change the whole course of my life.

Did not know it was the rush hour.
Should've warned me,
Should've
Should've warned me.

Veronica Williams

Nobody

Nobody could touch me.
Nobody was allowed to.
Then why had he placed his hand there?
Was he allowed to because he was nobody? Was he?

Was it all right?
I'm not quite sure.
I'm not quite ten yet.
He is one hundred.
Why do my lips burn?
He is nobody.
Nobody's allowed to touch my lips.

We have to clean out the art room.
Girls clean out the art room.
Boys play football.
Nobody sees me walking though the corridor.
Nobody hurts me for walking through the corridor.
I tell nobody I have to tidy the art room.
Nobody told me so.

The art room is at the other end of the corridor.
The boys are playing football.
Nobody is supervising the football.
Is spying us through the window in the corridor
on our way to clean the art room.

How can we get from the classroom to the art room
if we are not allowed to walk through the corridor.

I know no other way.
She knows no other way.
We know no other way.
There must be another way.
Nobody seems to know.
Nobody tells us nothing something nothing . . .

Nobody hurts us.
We don't like nobody.
Nobody likes us.

Brenda Agard

I Love You It's True

I love you it's true but is there anything in that?
I love baked potatoes and cheese,
Nice ripe red tomatoes and salad cream.
But does that mean anything?
Our tastes change and then infatuation . . .
Boredom sets in
And I must try something new.
But I love you and I loved Curly-Wurlys,
Mars bars and Fry's Turkish Delight.
Now my sweet tooth is dead.
I love you it's true but is there anything in that?

Carole Stewart

How Times Have Changed!

I remember how
in days long ago
I would
squeeze my eyes tight shut
and pray
tremblingly
lord
let this relationship
work out
even though
he's awful sometimes
you know
that truly
he's beautiful
lord
bring out
the best in him
make him be really
beautiful
lord
make this relationship
work out

and sometimes
I even added
threateningly
or i shall die

and waited for results

perhaps i hoped
that man to man
they'd work it out
and perhaps
they did

How times have changed!

now
meeting you
whom I quite fancy
I say simply
to the watching me

seems to me
it would be quite nice
if something works
but I suspect
he can be quite awful
if so
just let him pass on
I'll survive
without the hassle

being lonely
when alone
can be quite pleasant
sometimes
loneliness when in company
is a pain
I've learnt to fear

if he's beautiful
let him pause
if he's as awful
as I suspect
I'll survive
without the hassle

from that
to this
from then
to now
it's funny
and beautifully peaceful
the way times have changed.

Merle Collins

Jerry Perm Poem

The sky was a bluey blue.
Sun high in the heavens sunning the earth.

All nature in rapture.

It's a lovers' afternoon.

And you,
looking so cute in your jerry perm.
Strong manly arms
holding me close.

The stench of the activator
making me choke.
All that grease
running down your neck,
down your back.
And making you twitch.

Your face inclines towards mine,
We're going to kiss.
I see right up your nose.
Am crushed by your lips.

You search for my mouth,
lunge eagerly in,
start slushing and slurping.
You're breaking my jaw.

Absentmindedly, I stroke your hair,
Ergh, now TCB is everywhere.
Lost in my mouth
You don't seem to care.

The seconds seem like hours
Minutes turn into years.

And God he sent
No rainbow sign

but down came all the rain.

We have to run for cover,
take shelter from the storm.
From the safety of a canopy
We watch the downpour fall.

Thank you Lord,
with all my heart
for rainy afternoons.

Carole Stewart

For Me From You

For days and days
your words have poured and poured
words heard before
words read before
        of
how much love
how much care
how much sacrifice
so much how much
how much so much
that in my mind
i go to a market stall
and i ask how much
how much are you selling
how much am i buying.

After nights and nights
more of your words come
come proposing
come disposing
wine carrying* in three months
a son for you in nine
teaching job with midday break
a party for you and your friends.

In this dark room
without the shine of the moon without
your words come muscled, come rushing

---

* Wine carrying is a major part of marriage rites in many
parts of Nigeria. 'Wine' includes assorted drinks which
are presented by the suitor to indicate his intention and
finally to celebrate the marriage. The bride indicates her
acceptance by searching for the bridegroom in the
crowd and offering him wine on her knees.

a nice big kitchen   for me from you
a little car for me   from you
a trunk box of wrappers   for me from you
a fat allowance   for me from you
ALL you say, EVERYTHING you say
    FOR ME   FROM YOU
i go again to the market
where everything abounds
where everything is sold
where all can be bought.

there i see all markets i have been to
the Yoruba woman said 'KOGBA'*
the Hausa woman said 'ALA BARKA'*
the Igbo woman said 'MBAA O'*
so i see that some sell and others don't

And in this moonless room
i see what i am buying for me from you
and i see my tomorrow tonight
and i see the sister of my tomorrow
and i see the sister of the sister
of my tomorrow
days endless and uncountable
if i buy
my place for me from you.

                        Rita Anyiam-St. John

*Yoruba, Hausa and Igbo words indicating refusal to
sell.

64

Even Tho

Man I love
but won't let you devour

even tho
I'm all watermelon
and star-apple and plum
when you touch me

even tho
I'm all sea moss
and jelly fish
and tongue

Come
leh we go to de carnival
You be banana
I be avocado

Come
leh we hug-up
an brace-up
an sweet one another up

But then
leh we break free
yes   leh we break free

an keep to de motion
of we own personality

Grace Nichols

The Blue Flame

There was no fire
only body heat
sweat
and checkered glimpses
of the past
like a mirror
on my ceiling
Body heat
melting inhibitions
moulding your body to some
exquisite purpose
taking in the edges
of fantasy
and shaping them
to fit the deed
Even then
your fingers are clumsy
fumbling at the awkward
lock
grabbing the roots of desires
and stretching them
beyond your own reach
snatching at illusions
trying to rein or pacify them
Enchanting
Calculated to moisten
the arid reasoning
it gives vain options and
fractions of hope
while paving the way for
pain
when
the blue flame
leaves you
naked and vulnerable

in the dancing labyrinth
of tongues which
lick
the open sore
stumbling through endless
curtains of icy transparent
shafts of elusive light
trying
to find your way
back

Amryl Johnson

Business Partners

We lie there.
I am asleep.
A hand runs smoothly over my back.
I awake.
A hand runs down around my left thigh.
I lie there.

My mind runs through endless thoughts . . .

Why am I here?
Why am I sharing its bed?
Why shouldn't I be here?
Have I the right to share my business partner's bed?

A hand runs smoothly over my back.
Has it a right to share my body?
I pull away.
It stops.
I move towards sleep once more.
It starts again.

My mind moves into endless thoughts.

I pull away.
It gets up.
Lights a cigarette.
Goes into the kitchen.
I cannot sleep.
I think endless thoughts.
I get up . . .
And follow it into the kitchen.

I say
'Let's talk.'

It tells me I'm inhibited.
I deny this.
I say we are business partners.

It tells me we should not have shared the same bed.
I say we are business partners sharing the same bed.
It tells me
If it had another room then there would be no need
to share the same bed.
Then it would be all right.
I tell it I don't expect to be used
It says I didn't ask for it to stop.
I say I should not have to.
It tells me
This has not happened since it was sixteen.
I say it's my body.
It says it will be bad tempered for the rest of the day.

It laughs and says,
the boys will wan' fe kno'
If im na get no pussy tonight.

We meet again
briefly
a few days later

I saw him at a function once

some time ago.

Brenda Agard

One Man to Another

said one man to another
I congratulate you
you have shown good sense
you sucked enough
of the water of your mother's breast
you have done this at the right time
at the splitting of head*
and you have got the right type
if any younger
the headache is too much
and if any older
they know far too much
this way
little education and body untouched
and eyes that have seen nothing
you have your own thing
make IT what you want
like a potter with his clay
so is a man to his wife
indeed shake my hand
you have acted like a man
like a true son of the soil
so that surgeon from my village
said to his newly married brother

Rita Anyiam-St. John

*Igbo idiom for 'an act of excellence'.

Picture of a Woman

Picture of a woman
lying on a bed
Enshrined in oil
outstretched and silken
an easy body – intact
he left no lines

Picture of a woman holding flowers
outstretched and black
outstretched to
body lying on a bed
head that's blurred and mirrored.

Picture of a body painted
Enshrined in oil
Picture of a lover enshrined.
A bed
A body – sinuous and black
His genitals intact.
A silken body through oil
sinuous and black – lying on a bed
Enshrined rectangular forever.
She left no lines
an easy body – intact
lying supine without a head.

Maureen Ismay

Beloved

I brought my love
wrapped
in cottons and silks
its face and hands
washed
clean as an innocent.
I cupped my hands
for love to drink from,
filled,
filled
with the sweet
mingling
of joy with fear.
I bared the red,
soft,
centre
where my heart had been
to nourish my beloved
and turn the hunger inside
into a field in harvest.

My love was tumbled to the ground
doused with the salt from my own eyes
then tossed aside in a careless gesture.

He who cannot accept a gift of love
does not deserve it.

Iyamide Hazeley

Once

Once I held a miracle
in my hand. It moved

Ever so slightly
redirected
by the air
around it.

Once I loved
as I feared
I never
would
again

Once I knew
the meaning
of dreams.

Maud Sulter

The Escape

'Who put the clock back, eh!!'

Silence. 'Who put the clock back? If me have to lick every one of yu pickney dis day, eh . . .' Daddy looked into four pairs of eyes, each eye running water, set into four heads shaking from side to side in denial of the crime, four snivelling noses, four pairs of trembling lips, with slightly audible sounds escaping, but not enough to call attention to the owner.

'Not me, Daddy,' chorused four voices in unison. 'All right, me have to beat you all one by one to find out the truth den.' Daddy was a tall man. Well, he was tall to us kids. He was a red colour. In fact, he was part Arawak Indian. He had silky hair which he used to shine up with Dixie Peach hair rubbing. He was quite stocky, and his hands had a large span. When they made contact with any part of your skin, boy, you could feel it.

A chorus of voices wailing and shrieking into a loud crescendo. The joke was nobody had got beaten yet! 'I can't imagine how yuh mudder gone, gone leave me wid de pickney dem, bout she gone to see her mudder,' Daddy said in an incredulous voice. 'And me a tink seh is only nine in a de morning, and is twelve o'clock and I late for work.'

You can't blame my mother for taking off. She never deserted us completely. We all knew that she was coming back to us. If Daddy had been a reasonable man, he would have been happy for her to go home to see her mother. But he wasn't. Mummy had to sneak out like a child who is in fear of her father. My mother had been in Britain for twenty-one years and had never in all that time returned to Jamaica to see her family because my father would not let her. Mind you, he had been to see his family. When I think about it my father was an out-and-out bully. All my mother ever said was that she wanted a quiet life, so he used to abuse her, especially mentally, and she would let him get away with it. He would argue and want to start a fight. My mother would calmly ignore him, which in fact angered him more. He was a bit of a womaniser, and my mother was a generous looking woman, which I think provoked my

75

father's feelings of jealousy. And what with his guilty conscience about whatever he was up to at the time, he was totally unreasonable. 'Yu a get feisty, yu want come out and find work,' he would say to her on Fridays, after reluctantly giving her a pittance for housekeeping for the week.

I loved my father, but I preferred my mother. I loved her best. She was so understanding, you could talk to her about most things. She was quite a liberal woman, especially in those days of West Indian parents who had old values, and there were certain things you couldn't tell even your mother!

'My!! I have to pay the gas bill, the light bill, the telephone bill,' he would moan, on and on. One day I said, 'Daddy, you always say you have to pay the telephone bill, but we haven't got a telephone have we?' Bof! Slap! Tump! Skin contacting skin. Daddy's hand on my legs. 'Who ask you to fast in big people business,' was my answer from Daddy. 'Yu pickney a born in a Britain too feisty for yu own good.'

My mother was beginning to feel desperate. She badly wanted to see her mother, who was quite old and had hypertension, and my mother's fear was that her mother would die before she had a chance to see her again. It was very sad. Us children would feel at a loss as to what we could do. It was horrible seeing your mother pine away quietly. She would be doing some washing in the kitchen, and then she would look up out of the window and you could feel vibes generating from her, from her yearning to go home to Jamaica. And she would be transfixed, deep in her own thoughts about her life that she had left behind. She would say, 'The sky at home is so different, clear and blue, warm,' and she would tell us stories of when she was a child, and the things that she used to get up to. She would make us laugh with little rhymes she would repeat time and time again for us.

Mummy had a friend called Miz Ruby. She was deadly. She couldn't stand my father. He couldn't stand her. 'That woman just a look for man, before she go home and stop fast inna people business,' he would tell my mother. 'Yu tell her to her face, if yu nar want her to come and see me,' my mother would say to him.

76

But for some unknown reason my father never seemed to have the courage to say anything to Miz Ruby, which at the time I could not understand.

'Evenin', Miz Ruby,' he would grunt under his breath. 'Evenin',' Miz Ruby would say as she waltzed past him in the passage. 'Hello, Patsy,' she would say to my mother with a smile on her face, rolling her eyes back to indicate the contempt that she felt for my father. My mother would just smile back, and say 'How yu bin,' sweetly to Miz Ruby, and they would both laugh as though they had just heard a huge joke.

Miz Ruby was a big brown-skinned woman. She had incredibly large breasts. I used to wonder how she managed to walk around with them all day. In fact all of her was large. She was indeed a jovial person, always laughing. She even had a kind word to say to us kids, which was unusual, for a big person to acknowledge children then. She always brought coconut cake for us, which she had made herself. It was rock hard and sweet, and we had to dig out the coconut from our teeth. She never had anything good to say about Daddy. 'Miserable old goat,' she would say indignantly. 'Patsy me tell yu all the time, if yu want to borrow money fi go home, just ask me and I will draw my pardner money fi give yu.'

'No. It all right Miz Ruby, me piece a money a week time me get inna de factory will cover. Me have everyting sort out, no worry,' Mummy would tell her and touch her arm lightly to reassure her.

'Me nar know why yu stick with de old goat, but for de pickney dem sake – me understand,' Miz Ruby would tell her.

Miz Ruby was a kind soul. She'd got Mummy the job in the cake factory. Four hours a day, five evenings a week. At first my father loved the idea of Mummy working. He thought he would give her less money for housekeeping. He tried that the first week, and I remember when Mummy put the food in front of him on Sunday and he nearly had a heart attack.

'What dis, eh?' he said in a shocked voice. 'How yu expect me to eat dis! Dis couldn't feed a mouse.' He pushed the plate away and looked at my mother. 'But Alton, yu never give me enough money dis week, what yu expect,' she replied innocently. 'But Patsy yu a work,' he said. And my mother would go into a lengthy explanation of what she had done with her wages.

The following day, he would reluctantly give her the rest of the housekeeping money. My mother told my father that she was getting £8 wages but in fact she was really getting £12. I wanted to remark one day about this when my mother said, 'Chile, why yu mout so big? Shh!' putting her finger on her lips. 'It's our secret, baby,' she whispered, putting her arms around me. I felt good to know that I had been included in a big person's secret. The money paid for Mummy's return ticket to Jamaica as well as a little change for spending. It took eighteen months of secretly storing the money and goods Mummy was taking to JA.

Miz Ruby was the instigator and officer in charge of Plans A, B and C. All us children was excited to be part of the operation, and keeping it from my father was such a joke at the time, although afterwards when we got beaten, none of us were laughing. And the more Miz Ruby came to the house the more my father resented her. 'Dat woman is slack and out of order,' he would say after she had left. What he meant, I'm sure, was that she had sussed him out and took no notice of him. She encouraged Mummy all the more. It was Miz Ruby who came up with the idea to put the clock back. She said she had seen it done in the cinema. 'Yu know the woman leave the man sleeping in the bed, and take time ease herself out the house, and when him wake up in the morning and she gone, him tink seh it early and go back to sleep. Dis time the woman gone bout her business.' She fell about laughing. We all started laughing at what we didn't know, but we were always glad for a good laugh, especially if it was at Daddy's expense.

'Now Patsy, put all yu grip dem in my house, and I will come to the airport with you and help you and ting.' She nodded her head. 'Nar worry about a ting, if yu husband Alton find out and him come to me house, me will lick him in dat bald patch him trying to cover up, till him fart,' she said menacingly.

'All right,' said Daddy grabbing hold of Blossom who was the first in line for beating, which I thought was fair considering she was the oldest and got everything first. Pow! boft! thump! slap! Daddy was laying into her wickedly. Welts started to appear on her legs, from the leather strap which was well worn from previous beatings we had all received at some time or other. The way Daddy was going on you would have thought he was getting paid for it. He never did nothing for nothing. I hoped that Daddy would tire himself out and that by the time he got to me, who was third on the agenda for beatings, it would not bite so much. 'Did yu do it, Marcia?' he barked next. 'Who was it then?' he shouted. 'I don't know Daddy,' she bawled.

Whup! whup! whup! 'Yu liar yu,' he accused her. Here we go! My turn. 'Me knows yu is a little liar when yu ready, so me is not even going to ask yu,' he said to me.

'It wasn't me,' I bawled, 'but I know who it is' – silence – 'it, it was Mummy,' I said as matter of factly as I could. Thump! slap! 'Yu too smart fi yu own good,' said Daddy.

When he got to Cassius, who was already bawling and wailing and screaming Daddy said, 'Chile, what do yu? Me no touch yu yet and yu a bawl,' and he pounced on him. They were both doing a kind of Red Indian dance, Cassius to escape licks and Daddy making sure that he didn't.

Then we were all crying and howling, our skins stinging from the licks, Daddy shouting and barking at us. At the time, we weren't to know that it was purely his anger at my mother foiling him in her escape (cos she was too stupid usually to mastermind such a thing). He was deeply hurt.

Well, life has to go on, and on it did go. I felt at the time that I wouldn't have minded being adopted for the six weeks, even if it meant a white family. At least I would be able to have bangers and mash, and fish and chips. Blossom's cooking left a dent in my stomach. It was awful and the more Daddy beat her the worse it got.

Sundays were a nightmare. From Saturday we all had to participate in the weekend cleaning: pick up the carpets and take them out the backyard and beat them; mop down the house from top to bottom. When it was dry, polish it. Wash the clothes, by hand. Everywhere had to be spick and span. Daddy would walk all over the house inspecting it and if he wasn't satisfied whoever was responsible was licked. I recall Cassius bearing the brunt of most of his dissatisfaction. Daddy had something about him, concerning Cassius, I don't know what, but Cassius was always singled out for punishment. There was no playing out with the other children. When the cleaning was finished, we had to prepare the dinner for Sunday: season up the chicken, and boil out the peas, and get our clothes ready for Sunday school. When all that was done, we had lessons. My father had trained as a school teacher in Jamaica, but because the qualifications were different over here in England, he could not practise publicly, so he practised on us.

'Wot yu mean yu don't know the answer? If yu cut a orange into six and take away two pieces how much leave?'

'Hmm, three pieces leave,' said Cassius.

'Bwoy, yu fool fi trut,' said Daddy, followed by two heavy arm movements across Cassius' head. 'Go work it out! Me nar know wat me do to deserve pickney like yus.' I privately thought what had we done to have a father like you, but was never brave enough to say it.

One night, I was awakened by noises out on the stairs, so I took time and crept out and there was my father. I am sure he was talking to someone but I couldn't see properly, and it would have meant me going out further to see, and I certainly wasn't risking that! But I remember the next morning my father was a different man. He gave us sixpence pocket money which was way over the top for him. Whatever had put him in this mood, I hoped it would happen again.

When the postcard came, we were all excited by it, 'Look, Mummy sent us a postcard! Jamaica look nice eh,' said Blossom. Daddy came up and snatched it out of her hand. After he'd read it, he ordered us back to our rooms. Mummy had not made any special reference to him in the postcard, which put him in a bad mood for the rest of the week.

It seemed ages since Mummy had gone. I was frightened that she would not come back for us, or send for us to go to her.

One Wednesday evening as we came home from school, the house seemed different. Mummy was home. Well, pure noise was filling the house. Mummy looked different. She had gotten fatter. Her skin colour had darkened and her eyes held a look that I had not seen before. She had inner peace.

'Look at me pickney dem,' she said. She had brought back fruits and fish and clothes and baskets and hats. It seemed as though she had brought back the whole of Jamaica with her, and just for us. It was like a party. Miz Ruby came round and she was laughing and joking and asking Mummy questions about home, and when Mummy gave her a bottle of white rum, she developed a permanent grin on her face. 'Oh Patsy you shouldn't! You spoil me, but tank you all the same,' said Miz Ruby.

When Daddy came home that evening, Lord a' mercy, it was like fire breaking out. 'Who tell yu seh yu can go a Jamaica,' shouted Daddy to Mummy. 'Yu tink seh yu's a big woman.' That sounded strange to us kids. Mummy was a big person and she could do what she liked. My mother as usual never answered him. 'Yu wait til later, yu gwan have to pay for wot yu did to me, going off like that, no questions asked or nothin,' he said.

The police came. There was blood and glass broken all over the place. Cassius started to cry. My daddy was nowhere to be seen. My mother was very brave. She wasn't crying or anything. I couldn't understand the blood. She wasn't cut or anything. What did it mean? We'd all heard the noise and the shouting, even the glass breaking, but we hadn't dared go outside and investigate. But when we heard men talking we couldn't resist it. 'Blossom should go first, she's the oldest,' said Marcia, who was usually the most quiet one of the whole bunch of us. 'No, I'm not going,' said Blossom, cowardly. 'I'll go then,' I said bravely. I peeped around the door slowly. That's when I saw the police. 'Now, Mrs Hinds, if he troubles you again when you hit him with a brick, aim properly and knock him unconscious, luv,' said the officer. 'Yes, sir,' said Mummy.

When they had gone, Mummy briefly told us all the happenings. Daddy had made a beeline for her and she couldn't take it any more so she started throwing glasses at him and he persisted and then she picked up the brick which we used as a door stop and hit him. When Daddy came home he was like a bear. His head was in bandage. He spoke to no one.

I felt a personal triumph for Mummy – it would be a while yet before he'd raise his hand to her again.

Millie Murray

Mama

Mama
today it's my turn
to write you before dawn
I turn over at the third hour
of a day not yet broken
by loud crowing cocks
and birds twittering up
and the sun that set at dusk
is not yet ready to rise.

Today is not the first
I am now a customer to the hour
of three
there's an alarm in my head
that never fails at three
I pull on my trousers
pull over my sweater
and over all
your red tie-and-dye maxi
my socks and my sneakers.
retiring to the table
where I always find
sheets and sheets of scribbling
from mornings past
and I am quite ready to talk
silently on paper
or clattering on the keyboard
of my Corona Smith.

Today for the first time
I remember at fifteen
solving your one complaint of sleeplessness
telling you that insomnia is a
positive sign of ageing.
that I'd read it somewhere.
I recall our nicknaming you

our dearest mother rat
for rattling so early
breaking our sleep.

I now know I must tell you
that sleep is now a slippery thing
daily eluding me, avoiding my every clutch
as boiling okro skips smoothly off the spoon.

I am now
like mother like daughter
a regular rattler
me with pen and sheets of paper
you with scissors, machine and cloth
rattling is now fashioning out.

I now see the sameness of
your three score but one
and my one score and five
a restless rattling within
alarmingly motioning body
regularly preceding sunrise.

I know not now
if when I've sent you this
you will wait for when I come
and we can talk past midnight
or you will do your normal bid
and write me at three
a time that now speaks
of this sameness
that I see.

Rita Anyiam-St. John

The Inheritance

On the day I was conceived
    what were your thoughts,
                Mother?
  Did you:
    Think about the latest trends
    knowing your carefree days wouldn't end
    perhaps you thought of your boyfriend
I bet your thoughts were not about me!

On the day you knew for sure
    what were your thoughts,
                Mother?
  Did you:
    Think: 'Oh Lord it can't be true'
    worried about what to do
    wondering why it happened to you
I bet your thoughts were not about me!

On the day that I was born
    what were your thoughts,
                Mother?
  Did you:
    Think: 'What a terrible pain, My God,
    but the baby look nice, it's not so bad'
    Perhaps you just felt rather sad –
I bet your thoughts were not about me!

As the days and years passed
    what were your thoughts,
                Mother?
  Did you:
    Think: 'She is bright, so I am hoping
    At any rate I seem to be coping . . .'
    Maybe you were wondering, planning, supposing . . .
I bet sometimes you thought about me.

On the day that I conceived
        what were your thoughts,
                    Mother?
    'At sixteen
        The chil' have baby . . . like me . . .
        things have a funny circularity
        There is so much more her life could be'
I bet your thoughts were all about me.

Maureen Hawkins

Where Are You My Bright-eyed Baby?

Where are you
                    my bright-eyed baby?
dead and gone
                    a dead-eyed darling
Where are you my bright-eyed baby?

When the worries are on your mind
and the kids, the kids keep screaming
and hunger scratching at their guts
and hunger scratching, scratching at your guts
Where are you my bright-eyed baby?

A sad-eyed, dead-eyed woman
                    faded at thirty
Where are you my bright-eyed baby?

and mammy had said
                    she'd said . . .
she had so many plans
                    she'd said . . .
her daughter was as precious as life itself
the one who would escape the life
                    the empty rooms, the silences
the endless cooking of dinners, the work
          (she'd come overseas)
bright-eyed looking from an old photograph
faded and static – relegated to the past

her mother's voice wafted through the room
like forgotten scents
                    Where are you my bright-eyed baby?

and memory like tears came unstoppable
                    bag-eyed she saw herself

a frame of ribs a back that's curled
while the children screamed and the nagging
nagging of an empty stomach.

Maureen Ismay

87

She Lives Between Back Home and Home

She lives between back home and home
Frantic
Desire mingling with unease as she
carved a space for you
Kindled a spirit that would guard against
The despair of her life
And the desire for you to be
What she could not be
Frightened she pushed
You away from her
And frightened
Held you too close
Daughters were to give
Mothers
A sense of themselves.

Sindamani Bridglal

A House

A House full of loud noises,
rich smells,
painful tears and side-splitting laughter.

A House in which three families lived
tightly squeezed together;
We were right at the top.

There were two rooms;
A bedroom and a living room;
With the kitchen
on the landing
on which the heavy iron stove
with its black dutch pots
stood in all its splendid glory.

A House of running feet
on uncarpeted polished stairs;
I slipped once
and broke my shoulder
after having been warned.
I attended school
my arm in a sling
when the teacher was having
us act out some nursery rhymes.
Guess who was a blackbird
sling and all.

I remember flapping my good arm–wing
For I was dressed for the part.
I was praised most highly for my efforts
broken shoulder and all!
We did a lot of play-acting.
I have always hated that
nursery rhyme and blackbirds.
Before broken shoulders
and hateful nursery rhymes

there were the tears of my mother
as she was forced to leave me
with yet another nanny
soaking wet, sore and miserable
with nothing but a damp nappy
to offer me comfort and torture for
my tiny body.
This is a story that was often
told in that House.

A House in which my mother
went from being there when
we cried at night; wearied-eyed
and tired, but unable to rest
for her day's work had just begun.

A House where my father was busy
nursing and feeding
three young naughty girls . . .
'We have breakfast in bed'
I used to boast to my friends,
I was so proud; not realising
until much later that this was
the way they saw that at least
we had had something to eat
before school.

Mum would sometimes arrive late
and they would not see each
other for days and we would be left
to our own devices;
then I was in charge and they
did everything I said . . .
'Now it is time to open our crisps
. . . not that one.'
And I always seemed to get the most.
But we were never really quite alone.
The woman downstairs would pop up now

and then to check on us; but I had
everything under control for they
did everything I said.

A House where the black and white TV
sat royally in the living room
and where every week Stingray would fly
into action. Funny how you remember
it all in glorious colour.
There were Stingray lollies . . .
Teddy-Bear ones too.
One lunchtime Dad was on holiday
and he gave me a whole penny
in those wonderful days you could
buy the world of sweets
You know Stingray was my first
record. It cost four shillings in
Ridley Road Market I recall . . . as
if it were yesterday.

I tried to do all the latest
dances. Ready Steady Go was my
favourite show. I had my own show;
my sisters being the sometimes
reluctant audience.
I would turn my back on the
audience and then jump round
announcing 'This is the
————— ————— Show', starring
yours truly naturally.
I would dance and sing, my
audience would clap and cheer,
and if they had been a good
audience 'giving me lots of
sweets' I would do a couple
of encores.

There were my uncle's records

and the Saturday night parties
we children would run wildly
about the House; no longer at
the mercy of our parents'
code of 'dos' and 'don'ts'
for they were too busy
and we danced to . . .
'My Boy Lollipop'
'Twist Again, Like We Did Last Summer'
'People'
'Havin' A Party'
'Stingray'; well after everyone had
gone – only us kids left.

My mysterious cousins arrived one
night from British Guiana and all
we did was stare at each other
wary of making the first moves of
welcome.
We heard of 'Home' daily and dived
into with glee
the boxes that would arrive from
this far-off place crammed with
bottles of guava jelly, cherry
and sugar cakes, peppers, the
gold ear-rings and the clothes
that were always too small, and
the bad tidings always arriving
in the form of a telegram echoing
death . . .

A House in which during the night
my mother and I had to face untold
dangers as hand in hand we went to
the outside toilet in the concrete
yard . . . well, I thought it was an
adventure.

And at night as five people slept
in that tiny space, I cuddled with
my sisters; they would urge me to
'do the Boat'.
The Boat was our way of being safe
from the night's perils; our whole
house at the touch of invisible
knobs and switches would transform
and we would sail to Africa . . .
Yes Africa. For even at that young
and tender age we sensed something
much deeper about ourselves.
If Mum was not with us but at work;
her hospital would become a boat too
and sail with us on our nightly
voyages.
But when morning came we would
still be anchored in the House,
awaiting the new trials of the day.

A House near a park where one sunny
day I disobeyed the Golden Rule of
talking to strangers and worse still
taking sweets from them and was
promptly sick after having stuffed
myself with pink and white
marshmallows and I still hate them.

A House in which I tried to play
'A Big Woman' and was immediately
made into a tiny little squirt
with the dreaded blue leather strap.
When we moved from our second house
we locked the wicked thing in a
cupboard leaving it to the mercy of
the bulldozers; Mum found something
else and then there was always Dad's
heavy hand . . .

Playing 'Big Woman' was a painful
experience on some occasions.

A House where at Christmas the
living room was aglow with warm
and loud colours and the plastic
green Christmas tree drowning
with gifts. Where Dad always
prevented major wars from breaking
out as we fought fiercely for the same
toys. Mum never seemed to be there at
those moments; for these strange men
would come to collect her for work
the night before and when she did
appear we would pounce on her
tired body; uncaring, begging her,
dragging her to join in our games
sleep once more denied her.

The House still stands as a
testament to my childhood and those
memorable days. A little shabby; it
cries out for a new coat of paint.
The House where I . . . We had so many
happy and sad days; you know
I still have Stingray . . .

Sandra Agard

Nothing to Say

Girl tell me de truth – What I must tell you 'bout yu father?
That I don't know where he is now?
Well even if I knew I wouldn't tell you now.
What would you say if you met him?
'Bout how I does treat you bad?
Or that yu stepfather hated you referring to him as 'Dad'.
What I must tell you 'bout sex before marriage?
When you know that was how you was born.
How I can encourage you to do what only brought me scorn?
And yet how can I deny that it was the love for your father
that made me take the risk, but it was the rejection
by my family that made that young, risky, girlish dream
become a sluttish woman's nightmare?
And what must I tell you about war and suffering
when we carved our dollies from wood
and our brothers built us toys and thought
guns and dying was just a game?
I can't tell you not to go to college
when I know how I had to stay at home
to carry water and pull up yams
and go to the river with the other girls to wash clothes.
What would I say? Go and learn girl
but don't forget
where you're coming from?
Go and learn . . . but don't get absorbed by the middle class
perspective.
Speak up for those of us who never made it past primary school.
Would you remember the importance of me singing
'Hush baby hush. Your Mama gone to town to buy
sugar-cake and give baby nana?'
Go girl and learn. Teach yourself but teach them too.
Don't be forced back or out or to the side
or always in the centre – but be there.
Listen and observe. Speak words sometimes
and sometimes speak silent thoughts.

Speak actions too.
Speak peace and fear and hope and love and pain and sadness and joy.
Speak it for all of us who left our shoes at the school door.
But girl, tell me de truth . . .
Why you does make me talk so much
when you know I have Nothing to Say?

Monique Griffiths

Dying in the Street

Megga
>   your child dying in the street!

>   We ran to my brother
>   not yet sixteen
>   The men with guns
>   stood at his side

Megga
>   hugged him
>   rocked him
>   tried to kiss life back
>   into those still lips
>   saw the desperation
>   still mirrored in eyes
>   which would not close

Megga
>   held her head
>   her wail was a cry of the centuries
>   rising and clawing the highest
>   pinnacles of anguish then ebbing
>   away to mere grief only to be picked up
>   in some other womb
>   Only to reverberate in the bosom of
>   some other woman who sees her reflection
>   long and clear on a blade
>   random and merciless

>   The halter to strangle the instincts

>   Your child dying in the street!

Megga
>   knows I stand firm
>   when I say
>   it will
>   never
>   come to my door.   *Amryl Johnson*

My Grandmother

My grandmother dream to me
She seh . . .
         You tree withering
witness to the withering of my life
         among the city jungles
fix my uprooted space
         so that my young sapling self
myself buried underneath the earth
         in between the leaves
like old-time people
fixed to the places
         umbilical cord rounded in paki
         buried deep down underneath the sapling tree

She seh –
         come back –
         Those old-time people
witnesses of dreams
         coming from the old-time-place
and the old-time people
coming to the place
         and in spite of . . . the place
growing with the trees
speaking through the entanglement of leaves
         speaking of my entanglement
and does not recognise the spaces in between.

I live on the hard concrete
where the trees cannot grow
I had almost forgotten when my ancestors dreamed to me

The rooting of my rotted umbilical cord
         feeding my young self
nolonger up to my knees in earth
         living on the streets
enduring the madness of an alien self

My ancestors dream to me
        'Come'
and showed me the magic blackness . . .

Maureen Ismay

The Miracle

Before you were conceived
                I wanted you
Before you were born
                I loved you
Before you were here an hour
                I would die for you
This is the miracle of life.
The pain, so great,
was more than the throbbing of your final journey
into my love
But part of a process
that came accompanied with
New Life
New Consciousness
New Understanding
New Wisdom
A bigger heart
To accommodate
New Love
At last Liberation
At last Freedom
How special, how valuable
How close to all things right
Nine months of worry and expectation
Brought more than imagination can conjure
Never really knew
Until . . .
I feel you coming
I am ready for you
I am ready for life
I am rejuvenated
I am Blessed
with the gift of life.

Maureen Hawkins

Praise Song for My Mother

You were
water to me
deep and bold and fathoming

You were
moon's eye to me
pull and grained and mantling

You were
sunrise to me
rise and warm and streaming

You were
the fishes red gill to me
the flame tree's spread to me
the crab's leg/the fried plantain smell
                    replenishing replenishing

Go to your wide futures, you said

Grace Nichols

Breaking Out of the Labels

I first came to this country nearly thirty years ago during which time I have fallen into, fitted and resisted a series of multifarious labels from: a girl from India, an Indian girl, a coloured, a Paki, a black, a wog, an Asian, and recently graduated to becoming a member of an ethnic minority.

Recently when I was asked to give a talk as an Asian woman, I found myself reflecting more on what to say to fit the label than what to say to fit my own person. Recognising this deeply ingrained old pattern of label-fitting and label-fighting, I decided to embark on a retrospective survey into the meanings and effects of my labelled past.

When I first came to England it was in the mid-fifties. I was an eleven-year-old schoolgirl on my way to boarding school, and was, quite simply, a little girl from India. There was nothing to quarrel about there. Even the fact that I had not at the time arrived directly from India, but from Paris, where my family had found itself, having lost home and city to Pakistan following the partition, I was still a little girl from India. I knew that India was free, and that we were refugees. From my father I knew both the Bengali and English versions of the poem by Tagore which had become the Indian national anthem and used to recite it to rhythm as I played hopscotch on the Paris pavements:

> Thou art the/ruler/of the/minds/of all/people
> Thou/dispenser/of India's/destiny
> Thy/name/rises/in the/hearts/of the Punjab . . .

My mother always chose to remind me about being a refugee when she dispensed my pocket money: 'We are refugees . . . everything we have is by God's grace . . . we are lucky . . . must always share . . . and help others . . .' But I didn't really need any prompting by then, as it was always willingly that I would place the greater part of my money in the large Munich beer mug my father had been presented at some conference and which had since come to be known as my refugee mug.

London, though new, didn't feel strange at all. In fact it had a fairy-tale familiarity in my eleven-year-old eyes. I knew it from pictures I had seen, from stories I had heard and so many people appeared to have visited, passed through, studied or lived in it. And, of course, I knew it from the Monopoly board and the childhood magic that had been invested in the game through playing it with my cousins in the sunny Indian courtyards, sipping long lemon drinks and wrangling over the property cards. And I was pleased to find that even the train that was to take me away to my boarding school left from my favourite station, Kings Cross!

My cosmopolitan Quaker boarding school posed no threat to the three pillars of my identity: of being Indian, free and a refugee. And the three countries I flew in and out of so frequently, reinforced the meanings which I imbibed as Gandhi, dignity, and concern for others less fortunate than me. As an Indian girl in Paris, I came from the land of Gandhi. In India, I was part of a history and a caring present, and in boarding school, my tendency to the most enormous painful chilblains would invariably elicit tender concern from my housemother and reminders of my precious Indianness. It all fitted neatly and felt okay.

But the okayness of it all soon came to an end once I left the protected precincts of my boarding school and came to London. This time it was not to pass through as I usually did on my way to Paris for the holidays, but to stay, get a couple more 'O's, finish off my 'A's, prepare for an audition to Drama School and find a place to stay.

'Are you coloured?' said the voice on the phone.

'I beg your pardon?' was my reply.

'Where have you come from?' said the voice.

'From Paris,' said I.

'Are you French?' said the voice again.

'No, no no. I'm Indian,' came my reply.

'Sorry dear, but we can't take no coloureds here.'

Surprise ceded to shock, followed by indignation. A stink

104

bomb had been thrown open and without realising it at the time I had absorbed its smell, as for my next call, I said:

'Excuse me, but, I am an Indian student calling about the room you advertised.'

Admittedly, I found accommodation, then and later, without much trouble and as the years went on I thought I was becoming quite blasé. When one of my theatre landladies said as I was leaving, 'I'm so sorry to see you go, you're such a lovely girl, even if you are Indian,' I corrected her as I kissed her goodbye saying, 'No, no, it is *because* I am Indian.' We both laughed, she with tears in her eyes. But the blaséness was only a thin shell, that covered, and protected me from the smell.

And so it was that I came to fall into the label-fitting–fighting game, and in the course of time became increasingly confused and bruised! For being 'coloured' was a muddly business, making less and less sense the more I learned. I learned, for instance, that there was a gradation of 'coloured', that it was more acceptable and more polite to be 'less' coloured. Paradoxically, however, this lessness was not necessarily correlated to pigmentation but to something more subtle, like packaging and presentation and the sincere persuasion that you were striving to be less . . . than you were.

But it was a losing battle anyway – and in spite of my beautifully enunciated drama school diction, I remained 'so awfully nice and really such a pity that nearly, but not quite, right'. And to add to my dismay I learned that remarks like, 'If you cut your hair darling you could easily pass off for Italian, Greek or Spanish, and no one need ever know . . .' were said with the best of intentions and meant to be taken as a compliment.

India! Free! Refugee! Gandhi, Dignity and Concern! The three certain pillars of my identity started to become marks of vulnerability as additional meanings got grafted on through new tripartite experiences.

On my longed-for visits to India I was the girl who'd gone away, always a guest, a visitor from Paris or London, staying in other people's houses, fitting in with their ways. Around me

105

Gandhi was energetically being woven into the web of mythical meanings and symbols, being concretised into statues and stamped as a new road name just as energetically as his message was being forgotten. The poverty which wrenched my heart felt too unjust and belied all sense of dignity. And being a refugee, which I had understood as being concerned for others – now also assumed a new meaning: that of being uprooted, of having no home and no refuge of my own.

In Paris, outside my parents' circle of India = Gandhi and philosophy, I encountered *'l'Inde mystèrieuse'* – occasionally mysterious to the point of nonexistence. Buying stamps in one of the outlying Paris districts in 1960, I was handed back my letter and told: 'Simply India won't do! You must put which India: French India? British India? Portuguese India? . . .

In England, Richard Attenborough hadn't made his film and Gandhi had not yet been elevated to being more than a half-naked fakir. And India? Well . . . it had been part of the Empire, hadn't it? Was there anything else to know?

Nothing fitted neatly any more and everything felt far from okay. I flew between here and there trying to find the where, or the way, to make it fit again. In the meantime, I learned chameleon-like to change colours to suit circumstances.

'A Tiger is a tiger,' my father used to say, to remind me of a particular story among the hundreds that had enchanted my childhood. In it, an orphaned tiger cub is adopted by a herd of goats. He learns their ways, how to chew grass, and 'bleat', both of which he manages with some difficulty. One day a big tiger from the jungle appears and the herd runs away – except for the little tiger who stays and continues to 'graze'. The jungle tiger stops in his tracks, whereupon the little tiger 'bleats' him a greeting. On hearing this big tiger roars in amazement and amusement. The story ends with the big tiger taking the little one to a still pond to show him the similarities in their reflections; introducing him to meat – whereupon the little one discovers his real teeth – and finally inviting him into the depths of the jungle where he rightfully belongs and can discover the mystery of his own true self.

In travelling around and searching – for my tiger or jungle – I managed to escape the Paki onslaught and by the time I came back as a 'returning resident' I was part of the throng of 'invading Asians'! During my absence, however, more than the labels had changed and feeling like Rip Van Winkle awakening from the long night, I discovered that a whole new generation had come into being. More vocal and less timid than me, they had even assumed a label of their own, that of the Black identity.

It was like discovering a fellowship of little tigers like me, seeing reflections in each other and sharing a whole new world of common experience and history. I was initiated and introduced to new ideas – about colonialism, imperialism, eurocentricism – perspectives which healed and eased. The scarred and bruised pillars re-emerged: Gandhi; dignity; and a concern for others: a shared reality.

And now, suddenly to ethnic minority! Ethnic minority? Which one fits me? Which one encompasses my reality? And then next year what will the label be? Enough! I'm stopping. Setting myself free. No more label-fitting or fighting for me. Neither am I searching for tigers or jungles any more – just beginning to roar . . .

Leena Dhingra

Pretty Girls Just Are

Pretty girls don't talk.
They don't have opinions,
Nor do they indulge
In intellectual conversation.
Pretty girls don't think.
They never bother to delve
Beneath the surface of insincere words spoken.
Pretty girls don't care.
They close their eyes to everything ugly,
And never dabble in such trivia as politics.
Pretty girls merely look.
Pretty girls just are.

Bunmi Ogunsiji

Dictionary Black

I was looking through my dictionary
Just the other day
And in front of my eyes
Though I was not surprised
Was a list as long as my back
Giving literal form and fact
To all those words
Containing 'Black'

The first thing it says is
Opposite to white
I say to myself
Mmhmm alright
It says
Persons with dark skin
It says
Blackhearted – dismal – grim –
Angry – threatening
Black looks
Black marks
Black lists
And Black books

Deadly – sinister – wicked – hateful
All these words to make us 'grateful'?

A kidnapped Negro on a slaveship
Is a Blackbird
(I thought they did have wing
Eat worm and sing and t'ing)
Blackbirding is the trade itself
That gave these people enormous wealth

Black cap is what you get
When sentenced to death
Black Maria – Blackmail – Black Death –
Hold on a 'sec'

Let me take a breath
I haven't finished yet

So just for a lark
I check out 'dark'
Well guess what it says
It says Black
More or less

A Darky is a Negro
Not fair – atrocious – evil –
And the Prince of Darkness
Is the Devil
And of course
Africa is that continent dark
(Where all those blackbirds did embark)

You want to hear more?
Well, guess what else . . .
You can darken one's door

I knew next what to sight
So I turn to 'white'
All sweetness and light
Not a bad word in sight

This white race member
Whose burden is leading
Characterised by their civilised
Good breeding
Benefiting mankind
With whitewitch power
Superior in their ivory tower

There is no Whitey
Nothing distasteful
Only the Darkies are disgraceful

So, due to their fear
And their hatred

They have
On purpose created
A language deceiving
The whole world's believing
This 'Oxford Concise'
With its 'ism and scism'
And outright racism

While we pay the price
While we pay the price
(Like Jesus the Christ)

Sista Roots

The Word

Black is a political word
This I now overstand.
If I don't use the word,
I said if I don't use the word . . . Black!
It makes me no less a woman than I am.
But brings me closer to my Home Land,
             closer to my Home Land.
Afrika!
        Afrika!
                Afrika
Afrika!

Fyna Dowe

Shipmates

I watched him as he entered
watched how he sat there
hands deep in pockets
face clenched in total black defiance
eyes moving now from nothing
to rove in angry unconcern
watched how the lips relaxed
just barely
when his eyes passed my face
returned
relaxed
wondered if to recognise perhaps
with cautious smile
moved again
with the easy coldness
born of lifelong practice
born of practical experience

but face not quite so clenched now
for silently he had recognised
another passenger whose averted eyes
could not possibly mean
offence at errant blackness

and as I recognised and shared his pain
my mind wandered
to his history
to our struggles
to our beauty
to our pain

and loving him
I wondered
wondered so hard that when I looked up
the giant hand was pulling to the doors
as the train left my station-stop

wondered
went one stop further
travelled back with clenched faces
black and white
wondered
found no sudden answers
and wandered wondering home

Merle Collins

Beware of the Poison

Beware of the poison
It shows itself not in the width of a smile
Nor the warmth of a handshake
                    but lying deep in your being
Manifesting itself
Until I am convinced of your objective
                    assessment of me

Unfortunately for me
Dependent on your graces
Not realising your addressment of me
had its seeds in the crevices
of your history
You could only report
            NOT CAPABLE

Hazel Williams

Visual Conspiracy

Images flicker across the stage
Images flicker across the page
Images flicker across the screen

They are not what they say
Some are not what they mean
Some are not what they seem

It is just a screen dream
a visual conspiracy
transmitting lies
confusing minds
enforcing false mysteries
twisting and dishonouring history.

We must learn to read the screen
            learn to read the stage
We must look further than the poster or page
and adverts for washing powder
or the revolutionary toaster.

We must decode these harmful signs
that are invading and mashing up our minds
It's a visual conspiracy
It is not a mystery
Transmitting lies
confusing minds
twisting and dishonouring history.

Who are these people that
conspire against us?
And why do they seek to deceive us?
At the top of the list in joint first place
are the capitalists and part time communists
These include the multinationals and those
who worship that thing called money.

The politicians who lie and cheat

to get your vote in hurry.
The thieves of humanity!
They all use that thing called the media
The press, TV, radio,
advertising and certain forms of socialising.

They seek to deceive in many ways
using a tool of brainwashed
ignorant fools
this army is so well produced
they take all their cues
from their directors of injustice and untruth.

We must learn to read the screen
We must learn to read the stage
We must look further than the poster page.

We have to decode these harmful signs
that are invading and mashing up our minds.

It is a visual conspiracy
not a mystery.

Fyna Dowe

No Dialects Please

In this competition
dey was lookin for poetry of worth
for a writin that could wrap up a feelin
an fling it back hard
with a captive power to choke de stars
so dey say,
'Send them to us
but NO DIALECTS PLEASE'
We're British!

Ay!
Well ah laugh till me boushet near drop
Is not only dat ah tink
of de dialect of de Normans and de Saxons
dat combine an reformulate
to create a language-elect
is not only dat ah tink
how dis British education mus really be narrow
if it leave dem wid no knowledge
of what dey own history is about
is not only dat ah tink
bout de part of my story
dat come from Liverpool in a big dirty white ship
mark
AFRICAN SLAVES PLEASE!
We're the British!

But as if dat not enough pain
for a body to bear
ah tink bout de part on de plantations down dere
Wey dey so frighten o de power
in the deep spaces
behind our watching faces
dat dey shout
NO AFRICAN LANGUAGES PLEASE!
It's against the law!

Make me ha to go
an start up a language o me own
dat ah could share wid me people

Den when we start to shout
bout a culture o we own
a language o we own
a identity o we own
dem an de others dey leave to control us say
STOP THAT NONSENSE NOW
We're all British!
Every time we lif we foot to do we own ting
tó fight we own fight
dey tell us how British we British
an ah wonder if dey remember
dat in Trinidad in the thirties
dey jail Butler
who dey say is their British citizen
an accuse him of
Hampering the war effort!
Then it was
FIGHT FOR YOUR COUNTRY, FOLKS!
You're British!

Ay! Ay!
Ah wonder when it change to
NO DIALECTS PLEASE!
WE'RE British!
Huh!
To tink how still dey so dunce
an so frighten o we power
dat dey have to hide behind a language
that we could wrap roun we little finger
in addition to we own!
Heavens o mercy!
Dat is dunceness oui!
Ah wonder where is de bright British?

Merle Collins

Old Age Come to Us All

Old age come to us all
if you're fortunate

Lucky to have spent most of your years working
Lucky
To look at your acquisitions
Few
Lucky
To have held a dream
Quickly dashed by the colourless shores
Better to have invested in friends and family
So that the joy of returning home
For a visit; secretly to stay
Cushions the shock; struck so hard
Thrusts you reluctantly back
To Reality.

Old age come to us all
If you're fortunate
Luçky
To have a state pension to EASE the well-trodden paths
Of poverty
Lucky
To be experiencing the twentieth century joys
Hardening of the arteries, hypothermia, senile dementia
Better not to have believed in their coming generosity
Politicians them
Enjoyed more the fruits of today
Cause your future can
Keep you dependent on the independent
But mine (ours) is a bold vibrant spirit
Refusing invisibility, refusing redundancy
Old age is not unlucky card dealt
But it come to us all
If we're lucky.

Hazel Williams

I Remember

I remember
watching the women
with ground charcoal and leaves
drawing designs on their mud houses
rubbing round and round in circles
with water and wet mud
to keep the insides cool
and the outside smooth.

I remember
seeing the men
cutting down palm fronds
folding fronds over sticks each overlapping
and held in place with shaved bamboo sticks
climbing on to the roofs and pointing out
the leaks
replacing worn-out thatch with new.

I remember
during the rains
making firebrands with pressed palm kernel shreds
and at night hunting for giant snails
in groups not less than ten
or setting out basins of water under light
to trap termites that would fly at night
after a day of rain.

I remember
the wrestling scenes of young boys
from my village and beyond
and the day my cousin Chikanma
beat the lot and was nicknamed
the cat whose back never touches the ground.

All these I remember
having lived it and seen it

they are memories to keep
for none of them remains
all I can do is to remember, keep remembering them.

Rita Anyiam-St. John

Strangers in a Hostile Landscape

When people ask me where I come from
I tell them this story.

I was born in the Southern Hemisphere
in the early hours of the morning
when night exchanges with day
and the light gains ascendancy.
What I have to say is brief,
so listen,
and make of it what you will.

When my grandmother was a girl,
paddle-boats crossed the river
from the town.
They brought all sorts of people
looking for
God only knows what.
Unspeakable riches, I suppose.
Instead, they found sugar-cane;
sugar-cane and mosquitoes.
They worked hard on large plots of land
dem call plantation.
Slaves worked the plantations originally
and when slavery was abolished,
freed slaves worked the plantations.
And when they were decimated,
we worked the plantations.
We were called,
indentured labourers.

My grandfather sailed on the ship
Red-riding Hood:
part of a straggly band
of yellow humanity.
They severed the string
that tied them to the dragon,

and we grew up never knowing
we belonged
to a quarter of the world's people.

A damn plot you might think.
Yes indeed, it was called,
colonial-ization,
spelt with a z.
The prince of the plot was called Brit Ain
but actually, he had many brothers,
Holl And, France and so on.
They fought each other occasionally,
but essentially, they were intent
on making themselves rich
thro' robbery and by brain-washing us.
They stole from us.
And at the same time,
sung psalms.
Such sweet sweet psalms
and sung so well
wash the sweat and tears away.

After much time
and many millions of £s later,
they leased us back our land
through a deed called In-Dee-pendence.
This meant the land was ours,
but every thing we produced,
was theirs.
We even got our own leaders:
men of great worth
to them.

Meanwhile,
another plot called Imperial-Ization
had worked its way through the world
and the earth was carved up
and re-aligned.

Back on the Plantation,
we all fought each other
(with a little help from out side).
We squabbled over what would remain
when the In-Dee-pendence deed was passed
and the prince departed for home.

And so,
in the midst of the troubles,
my parents packed their bags.
They followed the general recruitment drive
to the imperial palace itself.

We arrived in the Northern Hemisphere
when Summer was set in its way
running from the flames that lit the sky
over the Plantation.
We were a straggly bunch of immigrants
in a lily white landscape.
We made our home among strangers,
knowing no one but ourselves.

When I was a girl
I lived in a box
that is why
my head is square.
I lived on jam
and played on the streets
I survived in this hostile landscape.

And when one day
I was chased from school
I turned and punched their teeth out.
Too harsh, you say,
I don't agree,
they would have smashed
my head in.

One day I learnt
a secret art,

Invisible-Ness, it was called.
I think it worked
as even now, you look
but never see me.

I was born in the Southern Hemisphere
in the early hours of the dawn
and when I die
I shall return
to a place I call my own.
Only my eyes will remain
to watch and to haunt,
and to turn your dreams
to chaos.

Meiling Jin

i wondered

i wondered
if in my sleep i could find that place
where the granary is not lean
and ribs not trying to tear the flesh.

i wondered
if i would reach the place
where there would be no one on pavewalks
hugging rags and bowls.

i wondered
if i could find that place
where the skies could not serve as roof
and the biting night winds as walls.

i wondered if the place was far
if the place was far
where the pekinese and the other hounds
would get more to eat
than the kwashiorkor haloed children
of the universe.

i was wondering
if there was a place
where all of us and them could smile
and
i was still wondering
when the sun came up
in dextrous turn
away from the window, from light.

i stopped wondering
i winced.

Rita Anyiam-St. John

'Silence is Nearer to Truth'

I handed my teacher a poem,
'This is not a poem,' he said.
'It has no form,
Your lines are unpoetic.
Silence is nearer to truth
Than your written thoughts are to verse.'
Feeling I had betrayed my learning
I laboured through the years to perfect my style
Wishing for the day when my teacher
Would recognise me as a poet.
Now I have little conversation left
I wonder if I handed this poem to him
Would my teacher clasp me to his breast
Or would he send me backwards in my craft
With the proclamation:
'Silence is nearer to truth
Than your written thoughts are to verse.'

Margot Jordan

Babe

Poetry comes best
in the dark.
It takes the edge
off conformity.
No worry about
dotting 'i's
or the look
of a word
or a letter
on a page.

No. In the dark
my dreams feel
at home. Out
they flow
untempered.

So having told you
why I sit here
in the dark
writing
this poem. I can
tell you how I
feel about us.

Shit scared babe
cos I luv you
See?

Maud Sulter

On Hurt

Hurt?
Who me?
Hurt?

Don't kid yourself.
I'm not hurt.
Just mad
at your middle class
pain in the ass
self-righteousness.

Meiling Jin

Nothing Said

We marched half the day
Until our feet were sore
Until the pain goes away
We will march some more

What do we want?
JUSTICE
When do we want it?
NOW

We felt for our
sisters and our brothers
who had died.
We wanted that feeling
to be carried worldwide

THIRTEEN DEAD
NOTHING SAID

We got our wish
But they got theirs
Next morning as
BLACK RAMPAGE
Was slashed all over
the breakfast table.

We got our wish
An inquest

But they got theirs
A verdict . . . left open.

We will march all our lives
And we will be sore
Until the pain goes away.
We will march some more.

Brenda Agard

Circle of Thorns
(*In memory of the New Cross victims – 18th January, 1981*)

There is a ring which shines brightly
It is the answer to our prayers
I am not afraid

There is a ring of rusty iron
which grates along concrete
until your blood crawls
And
I have seen
I have seen
I have seen the young willow
sink beneath the waves
    beneath the waves
    beneath the hand which does not
replenish
So
when they ask
For whom the bell tolls?
Tell them
        Male black aged nineteen
        Female black aged seventeen
Two faces
in
a storm

Amryl Johnson

Like Dogs

They hounded us like dogs
Until we took to our knees
Until we were ashamed to turn
our faces
towards the light
Our bellies crawling
in the mud
Hearts like festering wounds
festering wounds like cankers
opening opening getting wider
And
Oh God!
the stench
I can taste myself rotting
I can still smell the afterbirth
and
my
dead
child
I can still see the fumes
from the iron
feel it
hot
hot
hot
red hot
The pain
of roasting flesh

Molten lava running through my brain

Black flesh
like me

Forget?!

Believe me
If I could
I damn well would

Amryl Johnson

Black Truth

The wounded were coming
in their hundreds it
seemed. The nurses
would patch them up
send them back out
to the front

But they would come back
in their hundreds it
seemed.

The bell rang.

Come afternoon the
wounded were coming
in their hundreds it
seemed. The nurses
would patch them up
send them back out
to the front

But they would come back
in their hundreds it
seemed.

The bell rang.

I don't quite know when
the war began
I'm sure I don't know
how.
But the end I still remember
now.

I don't want her patching
me up, one of the soldiers
said

Why? said one of the other
nurses.
She's black, he said.
She's black, the nurse heard.
She's black and I cried

I walked away, the other
nurse she came with me
Never mind, she said
reassuringly
We'll find something
new.

But even then we both knew
Playtimes would never be
the same.

Brenda Agard

De Youths

Dem youths now a days
dem no skin up no way
dem jus a trod it inna
militant style

Some sport fashion
on social security rations
dem no care how dem
walk dem jus wile

For is style dem a check
not de YTS set
dem a walk an a show
nuff coil

dem a break dance
dem a robot
dem a move wid de
up town groove

dem a lyric chatter
an a wise cracker
dem jus a bob
an a weave
an a move

De youth man dem
chat bout girl frien
an how dem control
up dem worl
but de youth women
say dem an dem a no frien

For is big mistake
youth man a make
if dem tink de daughter
a bow

For de youth women
wicked and wile
always drop it inna a warrior
style

always de in dem own possie
Thru youth man
gwan bossie
dem no scared a treat
cause when dem get vex
dem prepared to put up a fight

So our youth people
a no simple people
dem jus need a positive guide
for when culture
come and dem dash whey
dem fun
dem will come wid a wickeda style

Nefertiti Gayle

Angry Children

Angry children
Standing on the beach,
Wild waves crashing at their feet.
Eyes set.
Teeth bared.
Angry children
Catching their breath.

Burning venom
Rising from the skin

Angry children
Crying within

Manacled feet treading the sand
Recalcitrant bodies leaving the land.

Angry children
On a cold grey isle
snarling and fighting to survive.
The land whose streets are paved with gold
where young Black mothers and fathers grow old.
Estranged heads and estranged souls
filling and cramming Their Mental Homes.
Disfigured spirits and broken hearts
Scattered lives from shattered dreams
On a cold grey isle
A displaced race.

Angry children
Not chewing the cud.
      Cold dark eyes are calling for blood
      Cold Black feet not marching for fun
      Cold Black hands are holding a gun.
On our backs the West was won.
Now for the West,
The time has come.

Your bastard seed
                now
Points the gun.

Carole Stewart

Guess Who!

South Afrikan
Brothers and sisters
They're starving and covered in blisters

Guess who a eat?

Digging down the mine
Fe mek a gold cup
Many go down
Only some
Come up

Guess who a drink?

We digging
Tomorrow's graves
Today
Kneeling beside them
A wail an'
A pray

Guess who a laugh?

Man never see 'im family
From year to year
'im live with other man
In a six foot square

Guess who happy?

A mama feedin' baby
Fe the so called
    'lady'
While she own
Flesh and blood
Have fe rummage
In the mud

Guess who guilty?

An upsurge
In South Afrika
The time and
The place is right
Rise up and kiss
South Afrika
We have fe win
This fight

Guess who scared?
Guess who dared?

Sista Roots

Disaster

When the nuclear disaster comes
I don't know whether
I might have the strength
to run for cover.

For by this time
I shall be dying
of bad housing
bad diet
complete lassitude
and madness
too weak even
to hide my head under the blanket.

But when my body explodes
into millions of fragments
I'll be gone you people.
Just my dust will remain
to choke you.

Meiling Jin

144

De Bubble Burs

De bubble still a bubble now de bubble burs,
an tings in de Caribbean are bound to get worse
islan' against islan' ina disarray,
an dem a rub shoulders in de American way.

Some say dis an some say dat!
Instead dem stick together dem a mount attack!
Dem say dem democratic an no want no Russian in de attack,
But still dem a rub shoulder in de American way.

Instead dem stick together dem a mount attack,
dem big shot action sure to break dem back.

De power elite is dey pon top,
Dem dress up sweet and open up shop,
dem sell all de islands to Reagan and friends.
Me tell you it's de start of de end!

Fyna Dowe

For Michael

Mi cyaan believe it
Mi sey mi cyaan believe it
When yuh hear from the shout
One dead
Who dead?
Mi noh dead
Yuh noh dead
So who dead?
Mikey dead
An mi cyaan believe it.
But mi haffe believe it
For de newspaper cyah it
An de radio a shout it
An de people dem a wail it
An mi ban mi belly an mi bawl
For de preacher man know it
An im noh fraid fi sey it,
'Ashes to ashes, dust to dust'
An hey, natty, natty,
Dem bury a piece a wi culture.
'It's a hard road to travel,
An a mighty long way to go'
But yuh neva go noweh
For yuh foot did touch de road
An all o wi did see
Seh de road yuh did a walk,
De road wi shoulda tek
Back to wi roots an consciousness.
But who coulda tell
Sey de stone inna de road
Coulda have so much powa
Fi tap yuh from walk,
Fi tap yuh from talk.

Ten cent a bundle fi de callaloo, dread,
Ten cent a bundle.
But wi cyaan eat callaloo
Wey fertilise wid blood
An wi cyaan afford fi lose
No more prophet
No more scribe
For ratta ratta noh bring back new life
For de pickney dem a bawl
An de rent di deh fi pay
An wen wi lose de prophet
Only Jesus know de wey.

Valerie Bloom

Life in Uncle Sam's Backyard

Livin in Uncle Sam's backyard ain't easy
Livin in dat backyard's no fun
For Uncle Sam have a dang'rous hobby
Him love collect bomb, grenade an gun.

An when mi Uncle get eena temper
When him wan tell de world him hard
De fus place Uncle Sam cas him yeye dem
Is roun my way eena him backyard.

And mi cyaan do a ting bout Uncle
Him have de biggest weapons bout de place
For him always love fe know seh
Him come fus in every race.

Mi woulda like fi tek a stand
An exert mi own authority
Mi come of age, but when him throw dat grenade
A wha a go happen to mi?

An a so him interfering
Him wan fe pick an choose mi fren
An ef mi chat to those him don like
Him mek sure mi no do it again

Him tek some o him collection
An tes dem out by him backdoor
Or else him henchmen dem come visit
An gently advise mi nuffe see mi fren no more.

Any rubbish Uncle wan dump
Yuh noh haffe ask whey im a go
Only de bes fe Uncle fambly
Wid fe mi fambly anything wi do.

Den Uncle Sam jus love fi dabble
Him have a finger in every pie
An when him decide fi try out commerce

Guess a who him tell fi buy!

Mi fine some ore eena mi garden
Was tinking bout sending it fi process abroad
Uncle Sam jump een tek ova
Say, 'It was found in my backyard.'

Him tell mi, mi shoulda happy
Him teckin such good care o mi
An mi haffi count mi blessing
When mi memba cousin Nicky

Since mi little, mi noh frighten Uncle
Jus as long as mi keep in step.
But Nicky bigger, an wus dan dat
Him living pon Uncle Sam doorstep.

An dat man act like him a God
In everything but name
Mi jus a wait fi de hallelujah
When God get tired o de game.

Valerie Bloom

Watchers and Seekers

Squared
within the vast
and smaller angles
which line the walls
a gallery of eyes
which do not sleep
follow the range of sounds
which rise and fall
direct against their vision

Unchecked
the seekers come forward
stop
move on
come back to stand
in trance
before the scenes from
other people's lives
held in trust

Committed
to defence which stands
at a tangent to the
main field of interest
guards hold ground
seemingly oblivious
to the strength
of their shadow role as
surrogates for interaction

This is balance
of an intricate kind

Amryl Johnson

The Great Escape

Fifteen million
Dead souls
    Alive
Never thought
They would
    Survive
Come back again
To clean the stain
    Left behind
Come back again
To heal the strain
    In your mind
Go forward again
And you will find
    Fifteen million

You'll see those slaves
Are not in their graves

Sista Roots

When You Have Emptied Our Calabashes

When you have emptied our calabashes
into your porcelain bowls overflowing
the surplus spilling and seeping
into foreign soil
when you have cleaved the heads of our young
and engraved upon the soft papyrus there
an erasure of our past
having built edifices to your lies
filled them with so many bad books and distorts
and sealed the cracks in the structure
with some synthetic daub,
when you stock and pile arms
and talk about the nuclear theatre
want to make the world your stage
limiting the chance of world survival
it confirms your calculations, your designs
your ambitions which we'll thwart
which we'll resist
which we'll fight in all manner of ways.

We will rebuild
we will choose our most knowing
most eloquent old women
to spit in the mouths
of the newborn babies
so that they will remember
and be eloquent also
and learn well
the lessons of the past
to tell their own grandchildren
so that if you come again
in another time
with your trinkets and arms
with porcelain bowls

and scriptures
they will say
we know you.

Iyamide Hazeley

Notes on the Contributors

Sandra Agard is a member of Obatala Press Collective. She has been published previously in several anthologies, and is presently writer-in-residence at the London Borough of Newham. She holds workshops in story-telling, drama and dance, and in August 1986 co-wrote the play *Women and Sisters* for The Royal Court Young People's Theatre.

Brenda Agard has been active in community work, freelance photography and drama.

Valerie Bloom was born in Jamaica, and studied English with African and Caribbean Studies at the University of Kent. She has been published in several anthologies. Her first book of poetry, *Touch Mi, Tell Mi*, was published by Bogle L'Ouverture in 1983. She is presently working as Multi-cultural Arts Officer with Northwest Arts, based in Manchester.

Sindamani Bridglal was born in Guyana, and emigrated to England with her family at the age of nine. She is a film-maker, currently living and working in Britain.

Debjani Chatterjee was born in Delhi, India, and was educated in Japan, Bangladesh, India, Hong Kong, Egypt, and Britain. She is author of *The Role of Religion in* A Passage to India, published by Writers Workshop, Calcutta, in 1984.

Leena Dhingra was born in India. Her parents came to Europe following the Partition in 1947. She grew up and was educated in India, England, France, Switzerland, Belgium, and has studied Drama, Cinematography, English. She has worked as an

154

actress, film technician, researcher and teacher, and is a member of Asian Women Writers' group.

Fyna Dowe works in several different mediums – painting, drawing, printing, music, poetry, textiles, fashion. She studied Art and Three Dimensional Design at Middlesex Polytechnic and Art and Design at The Institute of Education, University of London. She is a member of Lioness Chant, which has performed its poetry in venues throughout England and in Europe.

Nefertiti Gayle is a member of Lioness Chant. She has also worked for a number of years as a Youth and Community Worker.

Monique Griffiths is presently a freelance journalist who regularly reviews Black theatre, dance and cinema for the publication *Spare Rib*. She also trained as a radio journalist.

Maureen Hawkins is a founder member of Munirah Theatre Company. She has been involved in community theatre since 1979, and has performed widely with various theatre groups.

Iyamide Hazeley received a Minority Rights Group/Minority Arts Advisory Service award for poetry in 1984. She was a joint winner of the GLC Black Experience Filmscript Competition in 1986.

Maureen Ismay emigrated to England from Jamaica as a child. She has spent most of her life in England, and is interested in various aspects of art – visual and literary. She now lives in South London.

Meiling Jin was born in 1956 in Guyana of Chinese parents. She emigrated to England as a child. She has wide and varied interests: is a black belt in Karate and enjoys T'ai Chi. She has written several children's stories and is presently working on a children's novel. Some of her writing has previously appeared in the *Funky Black Women's Journal*. A collection of her poetry, *Gifts from my Grandmother*, was published in 1985 by Sheba Feminst Publishers.

Amryl Johnson was born in Trinidad, and studied African and Caribbean Studies at the University of Kent. Her poetry and prose have been published previously in several anthologies. She regularly reads her work in venues throughout Britain.

Margot Jordan was born in 1955 in Barbados, and emigrated to England with her parents in 1964. Her work has been published previously in several magazines.

Millie Murray was born in London, in 1958, of Jamaican parentage. A qualified nurse, she has attended drama college and worked with several Black theatre workshops. She has been vocalist with various groups, including a gospel choir, and is presently co-writing, with Sandra Agard, a play on the lives of Billie Holiday and Bessie Smith.

Grace Nichols grew up in Guyana, and emigrated to Britain in 1977. She has published a number of children's books including *Leslyn in London*, published by Hodder. Her cycle of poems *I is a Long Memoried Woman* won the Commonwealth Poetry Prize in 1982 and her collection *The Fat Black Woman's Poems* was among the first titles from Virago Poets. She has just published her first adult novel, *Whole of a Morning Sky*, set in Guyana (Virago, 1986).

Bunmi Ogunsiji, aged 20, is presently studying Drama/Educational Studies. She has worked, she says, as a ('totally incompetent') crew member of MacDonald's, as a clerical assistant ('one day was enough!') and as a painter and decorator ('one unique experience I wish to God I could forget').

Sista Roots was formerly known as Ras Tina. She is the Chairperson of the North London (Camden) based Voluntary Youth Performing and Visual Arts Organisation. Also a visual artist, she works in rhythm and dance, and is a children's story-teller.

a-dZiko Simba is a founder member of Munirah Theatre Company, a Black Women's Theatre Company which has performed extensively throughout Britain. Her poem 'Black

Coffee and Cigarette Blues' won first prize in the 1985 Greater London Council literature competition.

Sherma Springer is a founder member of Munirah Theatre Company. She made her acting debut with North Herts. Youth Theatre in 1972 and later performed throughout Britain with Images Theatre Company.

Rita Anyiam-St. John was born in 1960 in Nigeria. She studied English and Literature at the University of Benin, Nigeria. She works as an editor and coordinator for a publishing company in Jos.

Carole Stewart was born in Wolverhampton in 1959, and studied at Essex University. She is presently studying arts administration at City University, London, and has published work previously in the magazines *Frontline* and *Middle Ground*.

Maud Sulter was born in Glasgow in 1960. A journalist, she also writes fiction and poetry. Her first collection, *As A Black Woman*, was published by Akira Press in 1985. She gives seminars and readings internationally.

Hazel Williams was born in London. She trained as a dancer at the London School of Contemporary Dance, and teaches dance at colleges, schools, nurseries and for Adult Education. She has worked as choreographer, dancer and actress, and is a founder member of Munirah Theatre Company.

Veronica Williams was born in Antigua, and has travelled widely and worked for some time as a reporter for *The Black American Newspaper*. She has had articles printed previously in several publications, and had work published as part of an anthology entitled *Poems of Time and Place.*

Merle Collins
Rain Darling

'Don't try to get me out, Tisane. This is the only place I sane, because everybody in here supposed to be mad: I like them; is the sane people I fraid. I happy here.'

In these haunting stories by the talented author of *Angel*, Merle Collins returns to her native Grenada to reflect on the ironies, the paradoxes and the tragedies of the lives of 'ordinary' people. These are stories to make the reader weep and sometimes laugh aloud in sheer delight.

Fiction £4.95
ISBN 0 7043 4258 8

Merle Collins
Angel

This powerful first novel from the author of *Rain Darling* is centred on three generations of Grenadian women.

Angel is a child in her mother Doodsie's arms when the houses of the white landowners of Grenada are burnt to the ground. Thus begins a thirty-year period of change.

When a black person is elected leader, the hopes of the close-knit community of Hermitage are pinned on 'we own people'.

Angel grows up to be headstrong, resisting the attempts of family and school to make her conform. At university, her radical ideas deepen and she returns home to share in the disillusionment at the abuse of power. She is reunited with her community in a passionate search for a role in the political life in Grenada – a search which costs lives when America invades.

Fiction £4.95
ISBN 0 7043 4082 8

Jean Buffong and Nellie Payne
Jump-Up-and-Kiss-Me
Two Stories from Grenada introduced by
Merle Collins

These two delightful accounts of growing up on the
Caribbean island of Grenada, one fictional and one
autobiographical, represent two very different voices: linked
by geography, and by the universality of human experience.

'A Grenadian Childhood' tells Nellie Payne's own story, a
child's-eye view of the Grenada of the 1920s, totally
credible, full of excitement, fun, dangers and occasional
pathos and pain. It is a protected, middle-class world.

Jean Buffong's fictional child in 'Jump-Up-and-Kiss-Me', by
contrast, is a village child, insecure but opinionated, and
constantly at odds with her mother.

An immensely readable volume, introduced by the
distinguished Grenadian poet and novelist, Merle Collins.

Fiction £6.95
ISBN 0 7043 4243 X

Joan Riley
The Unbelonging

Summoned to Britain by a father she has never known, eleven-year-old Hyacinth exchanges the warmth and exuberance of the backstreets of Kingston, Jamaica for the gloom of inner-city London. She finds herself in a land of strangers, the only black face in a sea of white.

Faced at school with the hostility of her classmates, and at home from her father, with violence and a threatening sexuality she does not understand, she seeks refuge in dreams of her homeland – dreams which she must eventually test against the truth.

Though academic triumphs help, for Hyacinth the real search is for identity and a place in the world. In her first book, Black novelist Joan Riley paints a vivid portrait of immigrant experience in Britain.

'Riley writes economically and with a fine ear for arguments' *The Times*

Fiction £3.95
ISBN 0 7043 3959 5

Joan Riley
Waiting in the Twilight

When Adella, a talented seamstress, moves to Kingston, Jamaica, life seems to promise much: a respectable career and the chance of professional status. Instead she falls for a young policeman who leaves her with two children. She is befriended and married by Stanton, a carpenter, and sails for England to join him. But Stanton too deserts her, for Gladys, Adella's own cousin.

She resolves to buy a home of her own, but is forced into sub-standard housing; in the end even this is taken from her by the council.

Now a grandmother crippled by a stroke, Adella waits patiently for her husband to return. Haunted by memories of the past, she assesses what has been achieved. Her life, apparently bleak, is sustained by her own generous love, and the warmth of her children.

This is the moving story of a woman's struggle for dignity against a background of urban racism. Riley pulls no punches in her effort to portray 'the forgotten and unglamorous section of my people' within a system which 'openly and systematically discriminates' against them.

Fiction £3.95
ISBN 0 7043 4023 2

Joan Riley
Romance

From the author of *The Unbelonging* and *Waiting in the Twilight*.

Two sisters could hardly be more different.

At twenty-seven, Verona is bright and capable but confused. Defiantly fat, she seeks refuge from a monotonous existence by imagining herself to be the blond, blue-eyed heroine of the latest Mills and Boon romance. Desiree is more level-headed but less satisfied with her role as mother to two spirited daughters and as unofficial kit washer for her husband, John, and his football team.

All this changes with the arrival of John's grandparents, Granny Ruby and Grandpa Clifford from Jamaica. The children are enchanted by stories of the Maroons and even John must jump when Grandpa demands that 'Oonu pickney must heed de older head dem'. Life in Croydon gets a thorough shake-up and both sisters begin to rethink their lives with unexpected results.

Fiction £4.95
ISBN 0 7043 4101 8

books for teenagers

Millie Murray
Kiesha

Kiesha has spirit, and determination . . . she dances in her bedroom with Michael Jackson, talks to herself about what her friends are up to and has tried — *hard* — to reunite her parents. But now that her father has gone Kiesha must give up her bedroom to her grandmother, Mama Tiny, who arrives bearing plastic flowers and a dusty photograph of a Jamaican husband!

Kiesha loves Mama Tiny, but doesn't want to be dragged to the local Evangelical Church . . . at least, not until she discovers that the music there sounds just like her favourite Michael Jackson . . .

The first pacey and spirited novel for younger teenagers by the now very popular young Black author of *Lady A — A Teenage DJ*.

Livewire Books for Teenagers
Teenage fiction £2.95
ISBN 0 7043 4129 8

books for teenagers

Millie Murray
Lady A – A Teenage DJ

August is fourteen and definitely not happy. She lives with her mother, her stepfather and younger brother, Troy, but she is often lonely and wishes she had more self-confidence. Her mother protects her too much, but is over-critical too ... and August just *knows* this is because she reminds her of her father.

She looks for something to call her own and her best friend Fleur, and an older neighbour, Miss Mercinda, encourage her to take a job at the local community radio station. And when she gets her own programme things start to really improve at last ... then when Miss Mercinda has a stroke, and August traces long lost relatives to plan for her recovery, her sense of responsibility really shows itself.

The successful second novel for teenagers from the popular author of *Kiesha*.

Livewire Books for Teenagers
Teenage fiction £2.95
ISBN 0 7043 4920 5

books for teenagers

Malorie Blackman
Not So Stupid!

Janet says that Susaine, the school bully, is an alien and doesn't have real blood . . . but should Ellie and Anita find out? And Jon has been getting at Maureen for years, so she simply *must* get back at him. And Tricia has died and gone down, but finds it full of people she disliked anyway, so attempts to get to the 'other side'. And Barry has been cheating on Margaret who doesn't take revenge . . . *or does she?!*

These unusual and often truly incredible short stories show girls who are ruthless and sometimes even cruel but never – ever – passive. Fighting back against schoolteachers, husbands, mothers and so-called friends, they choose solutions that most of us would not consider for tricky situations that many dare not even imagine . . .

Livewire Book for Teenagers
Teenage fiction £3.50
ISBN 0 7043 4924 8